WHY
PATTI
SMITH
MATTERS

M
M Music
Matters

Evelyn McDonnell and Oliver Wang

Series Editors

WHY
PATTI
SMITH
MATTERS

Caryn Rose

UNIVERSITY OF TEXAS PRESS

AUSTIN

Requests for permission to reproduce material from this work should be sent to:
 Permissions
 University of Texas Press
 P.O. Box 7819
 Austin, TX 78713-7819
 utpress.utexas.edu/rp-form

♾ The paper used in this book meets the minimum requirements of ANSI/NISO
Z39.48-1992 (R1997) (Permanence of Paper).

Library of Congress Cataloging-in-Publication Data
Names: Rose, Caryn, author.
Title: Why Patti Smith matters / Caryn Rose.
Other titles: Music matters.
Description: First edition. | Austin : University of Texas Press, 2022. | Series: Music
matters | Includes bibliographical references.
Identifiers: LCCN 2021048537 (print) | LCCN 2021048538 (ebook)
 ISBN 978-1-4773-2011-2 (paperback)
 ISBN 978-1-4773-2533-9 (PDF)
 ISBN 978-1-4773-2534-6 (ePub)
Subjects: LCSH: Smith, Patti. | Smith, Patti—Criticism and interpretation. |
Smith, Patti—Influence. | Women punk rock musicians—United States—Biography. |
Women poets—Biography. | Punk rock music—United States—History and criticism. |
Musicians as authors. | Musicians as artists.
Classification: LCC ML420.S672 R67 2022 (print) | LCC ML420.S672 (ebook) |
DDC 782.42166092 [B]—dc23
LC record available at https://lccn.loc.gov/2021048537
LC ebook record available at https://lccn.loc.gov/2021048538

doi:10.7560/320112

For my father, Jerome M. Rose:
He was a worker.

CONTENTS

PREFACE

It is December 31, 2008, and Patti Smith and her band are ringing in the New Year at the Bowery Ballroom over a three-night stand that had become a grand New York City tradition starting in 1998. Just before midnight, the band played "Beneath the Southern Cross," a track from her 1996 album *Gone Again*, the first record of the second phase of her career. "Southern Cross" as recorded is a hymn, a dirge, a paean; live, it embodies those elements and then Patti transforms it into something wholly spiritual and uplifting, never failing to raise energy from the music and the notes and the keening of the vocal melody.

Tonight, following a countdown to midnight somewhere in the middle — where friends hand out party hats, the audience blows noisemakers, and we throw confetti on ourselves and toward the band onstage — the final bridge of "Southern Cross," always a wall of undulating guitars and unexpectedly melodic bass, is the backdrop for Patti's improvised recognition of the election of Barack Obama to the White House, relieved and grateful, but still cautioning us to hold the government accountable.

This is followed by a hilariously ragtag rendition of "Auld Lang Syne," where Lenny Kaye, Patti's guitarist, majordomo, and earliest collaborator, tries to unite the band to sing in unison. He abandons ship when Patti vamps into "What the hell / does lang syne mean? / What the hell does it / mean?" Everyone, band and crowd, collapses into giggles. This is probably not what most people would expect from the "Godmother of Punk" but it actually encapsulates the average Patti Smith live experience perfectly: she can manifest moments of communion and rock and roll ecstasy and in the next breath, tell a joke or make a self-deprecating aside. In the process, she reminds us that our feet are very much planted on this earth.

The encore is the Four Tops' Motown classic "Reach Out (I'll Be There)" and in the middle Patti explains, "We have to leave because another band has to come on, so we're not gonna leave, make you clap, and come back. We don't want to waste the time, so we're going to do one more song. Hope you have a great New Year." She apologizes if she seems a little off, noting that it was very humid and hot onstage.

Any artist would be forgiven at that point for ending the show or throwing the softest of softballs to bring the night to an end. But this is Patti Smith, and in my experience, Patti Smith does not do half measures. So the band responds with a low, vibrating rumble as a backdrop to Patti's passionate invocation that 2009 will be a better year and that we will support and expect a great deal from our new president. And then drummer Jay Dee Daugherty ("My only drummer," Patti reminded us when she was inducted into the Rock & Roll Hall of Fame the previous year) strikes the kit with his usual crisp, martial ferocity, and it's "Rock N Roll N——r," a song from her third album, *Easter*, and a fairly usual choice for this point of the show. (N.B.: This is not the point in this book where I discuss the continued existence of this song in the set; I will do that later.)

I cannot sing the words to this song, but I can revel in its punk psychedelia, jump around with my friends, and be grateful that I get to experience this in 2008, twenty-nine years after I saw her perform for the first time, twenty-nine years after Patti Smith left rock and roll to get married and raise a family, thirteen years after she returned to "the family business." When she left us in 1979, I never thought we would see her again. I certainly did not think that I would watch her performing onstage at age sixty-one with the electric energy and verve of her younger years.

In the bridge, when Patti is attacking the strings of her Fender Duo-Sonic, she steps to the mic and delivers this message: "I hope you have a great New Year. Work hard! Don't be afraid to work! Don't be afraid of failure. Don't be afraid if the money's low. Don't be afraid to drink bread and water. It'll get better. Don't be afraid!"

It is as though she is speaking to me directly, and I freeze where I am standing. I have recently finished a novel, gotten an agent, and am now trying to get it published. I have received rejection after rejection. My agent has told me that this is actually good news, and I should "just" write another. I am in fact writing another (and would then write another, and start a fourth). It is a hard and solitary pursuit, and I work 9–5 in one job and then write in every other moment that I can. I was at the show for the reasons I am always at a Patti Smith show. I was not, however, expecting to receive what amounted to a surprise benediction from the universe.

That is probably the moment I first started thinking about the day I would be able to write a book on Patti Smith.

Patti Smith was and still is a hero, a goddess, a field marshal, a saint. She was also just an awkward, skinny kid from South Jersey. Whether we were from New Jersey or anywhere else on the planet, we recognized ourselves in her sharp angles and her inability to fit into the "normal" world. But instead of slinking stealthily through it, she insisted on being seen and heard.

For those of us who felt more comfortable around books than people, Smith made literature and reading not just desirable, but also implicit. Her initial forays into public performance were based on poetry, and she idolized Arthur Rimbaud as much as she did Bob Dylan. She made Jean Genet and William Blake and Allen Ginsberg common interview topics. She saw herself as the next rung in that ladder and paid far more than lip service to that role, both lyrically and in her continued work within the form. She still reads poetry onstage today.

In the 1970s, when Patti decided to head in the direction of rock and roll, there was a dearth of strong female role models in popular music, especially those who did not subscribe to conventional standards of female beauty. The gift of punk rock was that the artists made you believe that you could do what they were doing, and seeing a woman onstage not just fronting, but also *leading* a band, her name on the marquee and on the album covers, was a beacon of hope. The fact that she was a woman who felt no need for makeup or elaborately coiffed hair and who wore what she wanted onstage was not trivial to those of us fighting our way through a world of lacy Gunne Sax dresses and Jordache jeans, the style touchpoints of the teenage seventies.

You can trace Patti Smith's influence through the decades, even if she is — still — the lazy and de facto comparison for any woman in music who performs from a position of strength. But she was and remains an influence on generations of musicians. Michael Stipe. Florence Welsh. Ted Leo. PJ Harvey. Eddie Vedder. Carrie Brownstein, Janet Weiss, and Corin Tucker of Sleater-Kinney. Every member of U2. Margo Price. Shirley Manson. Sonic Youth. Courtney Love. The Smiths. Bikini Kill. Penelope Houston. The Raincoats. (This is not a complete list by any means!) When Patti plays a music festival, it doesn't matter where in the world it is, the wings are crowded with other performers on the bill, as excited to be there as the people in the crowd.

This book is called *Why Patti Smith Matters*, and the above paragraphs would almost be enough to prove the case.

But it would take a book much, much longer than this one when you add her influence over multiple generations; her groundbreaking, revolutionary punk-era career; her work that followed her return to the music business after the death of her husband; her poetry; her literary career (Smith noted in 2019 that "people used to come up to me and thank me for *Horses*, now they thank me for *Just Kids*");[1] her contributions to movie soundtracks; her charity work; the dozens of friends, colleagues, and supporters whose work she champions one way or another; her guest appearances; and her visual art. She is also continuing to adapt to new forms: within the past few years, she's joined forces with Soundwalk Collective, an experimental sound group, on ambitious projects joining site-specific field recordings behind readings of obscure poets, and she has collected close to a million followers on Instagram, where she provides a daily stream of consciousness about what she's reading, whose birthday it is, and what she's working on. In early 2021, she launched a subscription newsletter, which included both journal-like missives as well as a serialization of a work in progress, accompanied by audio narration.

This is not a biography and this is not a hagiography. This is a book about Patti Smith's work, because it is her work that matters, and because of that work and the value that she places on her labor within the creative process. The flier advertising the first performance she ever did, at St. Mark's Church in New York City in 1971, stated, "Gerard Malanga: POETRY. Patti Smith: WORK." The latter wasn't accidental; it was a completely deliberate choice. She has said that she hopes her gravestone says she was a worker; she has always referred to her performances as "jobs." This makes her unique in that talking about and acknowledging effort is not considered "cool." But it is yet another demystification that adheres to the tenets of punk rock. In the early days, when the Patti Smith Group would be on tour, she would say, "Next time we're in town, don't even come to see us. Be at another club playing yourself."

Patti Smith has always worked. She is still working. She has never stopped and is unlikely to do so any time soon. In 2020, she told *Interview* magazine, "That's what I think of myself as, a worker. The nice thing about that is you can be a worker for as long as you live! So, I never have to retire. I'm always going to be a worker."[2]

This is also the first book on Patti Smith written by a woman. This is not unimportant, even if its subject doesn't care to be defined as a female artist. She is a great artist, period, and it is high time her work was interpreted outside the male gaze.

— 1 —

THREE CHORDS MERGED WITH
THE POWER OF THE WORD

On February 10, 1971, Patti Smith stepped onto the platform at the front of St. Mark's Church, carrying a sheaf of papers. She was the first poet on the bill — the support act, if you will — for the Poetry Project's weekly reading event, on this date featuring Gerard Malanga, of Warhol Factory fame. Smith had been writing poetry since her teens — her fan club magazine would later regularly reprint pieces she had written while in high school, provided courtesy Patti's mother — and it was one of several artistic outlets she had been seriously pursuing since her arrival in New York City in 1967.

"This reading is dedicated to crime!" she exclaimed after her first number, which she declared "my version" of Kurt Weill and Bertolt Brecht's "Mack the Knife," chosen because it was Brecht's birthday, she told the crowd.[1] It was *her version* because the lyrics bear a loose relationship with the original. But "Mack the Knife" both warmed up the audience with its familiarity and her humorous interpretation of the lyrics and set her desired tone for the next half hour or so.

Patti read pieces about the devil, thieves, Jesse James, death, lost love, and outlaw, outsider behavior. She absolutely intended to shake things up, or at the very least, not be boring. The poet Gregory Corso, a mentor to Patti, often complained about boring poetry readings. She recalled sitting with him at the Poetry Project as he heckled readers by saying, "No blood! Get a transfusion!" As she related later in her 2010 memoir, *Just Kids*, "I made a mental note to make certain I was never boring if I read my own poems one day."[2]

As part of that commitment, Patti was accompanied by a lanky, bespectacled fellow on electric guitar for four of the pieces (although aside from the Brecht, which was less sung than *declared*), these weren't songs; the guitar was there for background texture. This was most notable during the last composition, "Ballad of a Bad Boy," a work that's always reminded me of a punk rock Edgar Allen Poe writing about a stock car race. The guitar player was a music critic, occasional musician, and record store clerk named Lenny Kaye, whom Patti had tracked down after reading an article he had written about doo wop music and suspecting she had found someone who shared how she felt about and heard rock and roll. She was right. The two became friends and would sometimes spend Saturday nights dancing to rock and roll records in the empty store on Bleecker Street. She knew he played guitar, and after one of her friends suggested she add music to her poems, she asked him if he could make his guitar sound like a car crash. He said he could. The two rehearsed a few times in Smith's loft on Twenty-Third Street, not knowing at the time that this was the start of a friendship and musical partnership that would endure for decades.

At the centerpiece of her set was a poem titled "Oath." The opening lines will likely be familiar — "Jesus died for somebody's sins / but not mine" — lines that would later be repurposed into one of Patti Smith's most famous songs, "Gloria." But at this moment, in February 1971, it was only a poem but still very much a declaration of independence. As she has explained at least once a year since she wrote it, the song wasn't meant as a rejection of Jesus, but rather as an expression of her desire to be responsible for her own flaws and failures. She was here to make her own rules, including bringing an electric guitar to the Poetry Project, something that was anathema in the same way as Dylan bringing a rock and roll band to back him at the Newport Folk Festival in 1965. "As this was hallowed ground for poetry, some objected," she explained, noting that there were "cheers and jeers."[3] Although she has never explicitly mentioned this connection, there is zero chance that she, a devoted Dylan acolyte, didn't take into account the parallels to Dylan going electric.

There's a surprisingly listenable recording of the day, thanks to Brigid Polk, a Warhol superstar who was fond of bringing her tape recorder along to concerts and other events.[4] Patti seems excited, cocky, nervous, and happy. Her South Jersey accent hasn't been smoothed out yet; she sounds not dissimilar to how she speaks today, just at a higher pitch and emotional frequency. She loses her place (a thing that still happens with charming regularity), she apologizes, and she asks for patience. But most importantly, she delivers her work with energy and verve, and the work—the poetry—is strong. There is "Oath," and there is "Picture Hanging Blues," still a fan favorite, a ballad of sorts written from the perspective of Jesse James's girlfriend. Patti reads "Fire of Unknown Origin," which later became the title track of a Blue Öyster Cult album.

Finally, there is "Ballad of a Bad Boy." It's this performance that stands out the most in the 1971 recording. It was the last poem in her set; you can hear the relief in her voice, which she takes advantage of to let herself spool out a little more rope, insert a soupçon more attitude, and hone her energy. The result is an emotional tone that is more playful, and it finally feels like she's having fun up there. She dedicates the poem to "Sam," the playwright Sam Shepard—at the time her boyfriend and the person she wrote it for—who was sitting in the church balcony. He was the friend who suggested she add music, who would shortly afterward replace the guitar she had given to her sister Kimberly with an instrument that Patti would call her "true guitar," a 1931 Depression model Gibson acoustic that she named Bo.[5] (She still has it today.)

She had not discarded traditional poetic form, but instead had created her own by hot-wiring rock and roll's energy and forward motion to the Symbolists' "mystical orientation."[6] Symbolism, the philosophy with which

Charles Baudelaire, Arthur Rimbaud, Paul Verlaine, Gérard de Nerval, and others of the *poètes maudits* ("accursed poets") were aligned, is pretty much what it sounds like: using symbols to stand for everything.

It's not that she was the first poet or rock and roll lyricist to use this method. Rather, it's her approach, her subject matter, her delivery, her phrasing, and how she uses her voice that make it unique. And the fact that it came from the pen of a woman is not trivial; I once wondered what it would have felt like if a woman had written and sung Dylan's epic work of symbolism "Desolation Row" and how that could have changed the world.[7] This explanation applies to future songs she would write, such as "Land" or "Break It Up" or "Birdland," pieces where it is blindingly obvious that much is metaphorical or symbolic.

"The atmosphere was charged," Patti later wrote of that day in 1971, and it's not an exaggeration.[8] The rest of her work, her life, her career, her contribution to the culture stretched out in an ever-extending arc from that moment forward.

Patricia Lee Smith entered this world on December 30, 1946, during a Chicago blizzard. She was the firstborn to her working-class parents, Beverly and Grant, her father just out of the army. The Smiths later moved from Chicago to Philadelphia and then from Philly out into the new subdivisions being built across the Delaware River in South Jersey. They settled in a town called Deptford, where the houses were built on land that used to be farms, near quarries, swamps, and overgrown orchards; at night you heard crickets, wild hogs, and other sounds that were more mysterious and less discernible for a city kid. Across the street from the Smith house, a local grange called Hoedown Hall still held weekly square dances. South Jersey is the land of strip malls now, but back then, it was very much its own place and not just a featureless continuation of exurban sprawl.

Grant Smith worked in the area factories, while Beverly waited tables at a diner and made a potato salad that customers would travel out of their way to order. Patti would end up with three siblings: Todd, Linda, and Kimberly. With four children to support, her parents were often out working extra shifts, leaving Patti Lee in charge. This might seem insane now, but in the 1950s, this scenario was not terribly uncommon. Eldest children, especially eldest daughters, often ended up in the role of supervisor, ringleader, and protector. Patti assumed all these duties for her brother and sisters, telling stories and inventing games based on the books she voraciously read and keeping everyone out of harm's way, as when fire broke out one night in Hoedown Hall. Patti ran outside holding her youngest sister, still an infant, and watched the flames leap into the air, an image that would inspire the song "Kimberly" on her first record.

Patti's father wasn't a religious man: "my father was searching" is how she described him.[9] Grant was interested in esoteric subjects that helped him make sense of the world, and he shared his inquisitive nature with his oldest child, who would stand with her dad as he surveyed the skies above Hoedown Hall, looking for UFOs. Beverly was a Jehovah's Witness and Patti's curiosity about the notion of God, prayer, and the soul compelled her to follow along—until she grew older and learned that the Witnesses considered modern art a sacrilege and told her there would be no place for it in heaven.

The Smith house was filled with books and music—rock and roll, opera, and classical—and young Patti, encouraged by her parents, found her refuge in all the above. "We were a very open family, where all of these things had a place of wonder," she said in 2015.[10] Her mother read her both the Bible and *The Arabian Nights*, which bookended a voracious reading habit. This was all the kind of fuel for a smart, curious child that would propel her forward and sustain her in low or uncertain moments.

Patti Lee was also one of those kids whom parents would refer to in hushed tones as "sickly." She contracted influenza each spring, and she managed to catch all the childhood illnesses of the day: measles, mumps, and chicken pox, as well as pneumonia, tuberculosis, rubella, and scarlet fever. By the time Patti contracted scarlet fever, it was no longer a major cause of child mortality, but it—along with almost everything else—kept her at home and in bed, suffering through high temperatures and hallucinations. The scarlet fever in particular she would later credit for giving her a kind of second sight, but she was already the kind of child a teacher would describe as "sensitive" or chide for "excessive daydreaming." She also had chronic insomnia and would stare out the window looking for spaceships and fairies while having long conversations with God. "I rarely slept as a child," she said. "Having God to talk to at night was nice."[11]

As a fellow insomnia sufferer, I would sit up late in my teenage years, headphones on, listening to her and others of the new guard, plotting my own escape, trusting that I would also, some day, find my people.

"No one expected me. Everything awaited me."[12] With that simple statement, Patti Smith described her arrival in New York City on July 3, 1967, at the age of twenty. She took the bus from Philadelphia to Port Authority carrying a small suitcase and wearing a long gray raincoat and black turtleneck. She was coming to find community and to find out if she had it in her to become an artist, but mostly to find work. She had lost her job in a textbook factory and was on the waiting list for jobs at the two other local factories where she would be qualified to work. She knew New York was full of bookstores, and if she had to have a straight job, working in a place surrounded by her beloved books seemed ideal.

The few friends she had who shared her progressive outlook on the world had already left for the Big Apple and enrolled in art school at Brooklyn's Pratt Institute. Although

Patti's parents were exceedingly open-minded for both the time and the area they lived in, it was still the 1960s and the career paths for women, especially working-class women, were limited. At the urging of her father, who was concerned that his eldest daughter wasn't pretty enough to ever get married, and "thought that the teaching profession would afford . . . security,"[13] Patti tried attending teacher's college, but was dismissed when she became pregnant at the age of nineteen.

It may have been the sixties and the Summer of Love, but in South New Jersey, Patti had to leave her family's house and go live elsewhere toward the end of her term so that her family wouldn't have to deal with the societal repercussions of having a daughter who was unmarried and pregnant. She chose to have the baby and give it up for adoption, but even after having done so, she knew she didn't have the money to continue to attend college, nor did she want to become a teacher. Like so many before her, a hopeful Patti Smith headed to New York City in search of work, but also in search of what she hoped would be her destiny. She didn't quite know what it would be or how it would manifest itself, but she was armed with the unfailing belief that it was out there, waiting for her.

Upon arrival in New York, she searched out her friends and played the time-honored game of rotating between couches and floors so as to not wear out her welcome. When that wasn't an option, she improvised. She often slept in a dorm hallway at Pratt, on the subway, in graveyards. It was a different city then, one that most of the world had given up on. As another kid from the suburbs, I completely believe her when she relates that she felt more unsafe walking down a dark, deserted dirt road near her family home than she did sleeping in Central Park near the *Alice in Wonderland* statue. I started coming to the city with my family in 1974, and it felt like large swaths of it — especially below, say, Thirty-Fourth Street — had been allowed to go to seed. In 1974, we were still a year out from the infamous *New York Daily News* headline declaring, "FORD TO CITY: DROP DEAD," but by the end of the 1960s when Patti arrived, the city had begun to enter the downward spiral that would lead it to the brink of bankruptcy. This helped create an environment where you could both easily lose and/or reinvent yourself. No one cared. No one was watching.

There's a particularly great passage in *Just Kids* where Patti describes what it was like to be in Greenwich Village on the cusp of the Age of Aquarius: "It was the summer Coltrane died. The summer of 'Crystal Ship.' . . . Jimi Hendrix set his guitar in flames in Monterey. . . . It was the summer I met Robert Mapplethorpe."[14] Listening to Patti recite that passage at a reading or a concert is always delightful; it is one of the many ways she keeps her friend's spirit alive, each time reading her own words with enthusiasm and delight, hamming it up for adorable effect. Sometimes she reminds me of Cloris Leachman in *Young Frankenstein*, declaring that Dr. Frankenstein was "My boyfriend!"

Robert Mapplethorpe, now regarded as one of the most influential photographers and visual artists of the late twentieth century, was, in 1967, an on-again, off-again art student who had rebelled against a strict Catholic upbringing and believed he was destined to be a great and successful artist.

He initially met Patti Smith when she was looking for her friends in Brooklyn and he happened to be living in their former apartment. Then, another time, he came into the bookstore where she was working. The third time they met, the Goddess got fed up and pushed the two of them together; Patti was on a blind date with an older man who was trying to get her to come upstairs and, um, see his etchings, and Robert was tripping on LSD and walking around the East Village. Patti ran up to him and asked him to pretend to be her boyfriend so that she had a plausible escape route. The two discovered they were both seekers, kindred souls united in their pursuit of Art. Thus began a creative alliance, romantic partnership, and devoted friendship that Smith would later chronicle in beautiful, evocative detail in *Just Kids*.

The Hotel Chelsea sits at 222 West Twenty-Third Street, a once-gorgeous ten-story landmarked building with an ornate terra-cotta facade, adorned with black iron scrollwork.[15] It is a *presence* on Twenty-Third Street, fully occupying three-quarters of the block between Seventh and Eighth Avenues. Among its many functions was to serve as a haven for bohemia, a refuge that across the decades offered succor to writers, dancers, musicians, and artists of all types and temperaments, and it was still going strong when Patti Smith and Robert Mapplethorpe arrived there in summer 1969.

Patti chose the hotel because they were broke and Robert was ill, and she had heard that you could barter art in exchange for rent. The people they would meet at and because of the hotel would end up being pivotal in both their lives and careers, and their time there would add to the Chelsea's lofty heritage as an artistic melting pot. But at this point, they were two hungry (both literally and figuratively) artists trying to make it.

She loved to sit in the downstairs lobby and watch the comings and goings, the residents who were behind on their rent trying to sneak by without being noticed, the new arrivals, the visitors and other more transient guests using the hotel as, well, a hotel. It was in the lobby where she would meet the archivist Harry Smith, where she would escort a tipsy William Burroughs out to a taxi, where Bob Dylan cohort and confidant Bob Neuwirth would ask her what she was writing. Neuwirth introduced her as "the poet" to other musicians, and through his aegis she would meet (and later write a song for) the great Janis Joplin. When Patti accompanied him to Woodstock where the Band was recording, she met the wunderkind musician and producer Todd Rundgren.

The cosmic requisition-and-supply atmosphere of the

Chelsea would also address more mundane concerns. The filmmaker Sandy Daley, who lived in the room next door, gave Patti carte blanche to come over and take a shower whenever she needed to, instead of having to use the shared hallway bath. And meeting fashion designer Bruce Rudow, another Chelsea resident, was immensely useful to Robert as Rudow generously offered advice about merging art and fashion. He would also end up with an oversize influence on Patti by later introducing her to her first manager, Jane Friedman. These encounters and others like them would lead to a spiderweb of other meetings and associations that would chart a path forward for Patti.

On the inside of Patti's left knee is a stick-and-poke tattoo of a lightning bolt. She acquired the ink from the Australian artist Vali Myers in one of those moments of synchronicity that could only happen in the Chelsea Hotel in its heyday: Patti was sitting in her usual spot in the lobby sketching out ideas for the tattoo when Vali swept into the building with a live fox draped around her neck. Patti recognized her from *Love on the Left Bank*, a 1950s book that chronicled bohemian life in Paris, and asked if she would give her a tattoo. Vali agreed.

This anecdote is fascinating for a myriad of reasons—Vali was an organic, fantastical artist whose work was widely praised by people like Salvador Dalí; the tattoo session was filmed for a Warholian type of posterity by Sandy Daley, who had previously documented Robert

Mapplethorpe getting his nipple pierced; and Sam Shepard tagged along and got his own tattoo, a crescent moon on the web between his thumb and forefinger. But the tattoo's true significance is Patti's reason for choosing that particular symbol. It came from a book she was reading about the Oglala Lakota warrior known as Crazy Horse. In *Just Kids*, she recalls that Crazy Horse had a lightning bolt symbol tattooed on his horse's ears to remind himself not to take spoils in battle, lest he be defeated. "I tried to apply this lesson to the things at hand," she wrote, "careful not to take spoils that were not rightfully mine."[16]

Her desire to get the lightning bolt tattoo came in the aftermath of the blinding success of Patti's reading at the Poetry Project. Immediately afterward, she was showered with countless offers: a two-page spread of her poetry in the nascent *CREEM* magazine and multiple entreaties from rock impresario Steve Paul. He offered to curate a band for her, have one of his up-and-coming stars write songs with her, or just to sign a record contract with her. She believed that Paul's enthusiasm for her talent was 100 percent genuine, but as she told the music writer Lisa Robinson, who became a constant and thoughtful supporter of Smith's work through the years, "I don't think he understood it, but he understands applause."[17] Ultimately, Patti convinced Paul to hire her as an office assistant, mostly so she could quit her bookstore job. "Steve kept asking why I chose to make his lunch and clean his birdcages instead of making a record," she writes. "I didn't really believe I was destined to clean the cage, but I also knew it wasn't right to take the contract."[18]

Specifically, Patti felt that her instant success wasn't sufficiently hard-won, that the people whose work she admired most, like her beloved poets or even her partner-in-crime Robert Mapplethorpe, had put in the actual effort. It all comes back to her belief in work and the importance of putting in the time and effort required. Patti Smith would have hardly been the first person to come to New York City in search of something, only to have it handed to her on a silver platter, but she was the rare individual who didn't jump at the chance. This wasn't because of imposter syndrome, nor was it even self-doubt. It came from a deep inner belief system and the work ethic instilled in her childhood. It would serve her well.

She accepted two offers after the St. Mark's reading: an agreement with Telegraph Books to publish a chapbook of her poems and a friendship with the music writer/producer/manager Sandy Pearlman, at the time working with a band called Stalk-Forrest Group, later known as Blue Öyster Cult. *Seventh Heaven* was published by Telegraph in 1972, and to promote the book, the publisher brought her to the United Kingdom for the first time for readings in London, which exposed her to a brand-new audience who would stay loyal for a lifetime. Her association with Pearlman led to her writing or cowriting multiple songs for

BÖC and introduced her to the band's keyboardist, Allen Lanier, with whom she would share one of her most significant relationships.

Jane Friedman is one of those names music aficionados know if they're the kind of people who read liner notes. Among her many credits, her publicity firm managed the PR for the original Broadway production of *Hair* as well as for the 1969 Woodstock festival and represented artists such as Frank Zappa, Jimi Hendrix, and Stevie Wonder. Her focus has always been on her artists, and she's given only one interview over the course of her career, which is unfortunate because her contributions to the culture have been formidable.

In an industry that doesn't love women in positions of authority of any kind and to this day defaults to the assumption that a woman backstage (or anywhere around music, really) is there because she has some kind of prurient motive, Friedman's portfolio was impeccable and impressive. After the initial introduction from Bruce Rudow, the two women became friendly and eventually joined forces as manager and artist.

Friedman had worked with poets so she knew how to find them gigs, even if Patti's way of reading her work wasn't like anyone else's. At the time, Friedman was also booking the Mercer Arts Center. The Mercer was a semi-magical wreck of a place on Broadway and West Third Street in the Village that had become a locus for performers and musicians who didn't have a space within the mainstream music business because of how they looked, how they sounded, or a combination of the two.

Friedman put Patti on bills "opening" for proto-glam bands that had their own followings, like Ruby and the Rednecks or Teenage Lust. She made five dollars a night (which she only realized later was coming out of Friedman's own pocket) with an act that consisted of the poems she had read at St. Mark's Church along with some of her newer work, sometimes singing, but always sparring with the glittery teens in the audience who heckled her mercilessly. She had to be sharp and she had to be good and she had to be funny, or she wouldn't have survived. This is where she honed her ability to manage an audience, a skill she would later attribute to her years of watching Johnny Carson, though I also recognize both the New Jersey in it as well as the weird kid's comedy defense mechanism.

The kid from the (actual) swamps of Jersey won them over; the audience would shout requests at her, poems they wanted to hear, like she was a rock and roll band and they wanted to make sure she played their favorite song. As the run progressed, Patti introduced a new poem she had written: "Piss Factory," the story of her escape from New Jersey to the Big Apple. "It seemed to bring the audience and me together," she noted in *Just Kids*.[19]

By early 1973, Patti had graduated from the Mercer to opening for the outrageous rock and roll glamsters, the

New York Dolls, at Max's Kansas City. The infamous back room of the club was where she and Robert Mapplethorpe attempted (and succeeded) to establish themselves in the NYC downtown scene. Now Patti was back, on the bill as an artist rather than a striving scenester.

Patti knew she liked being onstage but didn't like acting. She hadn't stopped drawing, but it wasn't compelling her sufficiently to be her main outlet. Patti had kept her focus on her poetry and how she presented it. She now had her first chapbook, *Seventh Heaven*, as part of her arsenal of material, which contained "Fire of Unknown Origin," two poems about Amelia Earhart, and one of my favorites, "Dog Dream," which begins:

> have you seen
> dylan's dog
> it got wings
> it can fly[20]

The poem then goes on to talk about Dylan's snake and Dylan's bird in a playful and lighthearted tone, sometimes sung as high and lonesome blues. "Dog Dream" was part of a reading she did at St. Mark's Church in April 1972, supporting her friend Jim Carroll, another poet who had rock and roll in his blood and liked to break the rules. (The two were briefly involved, but their mutual admiration of each other's work long outlasted their romantic entanglement.) At that reading, Patti declared:

This reading is dedicated to Smokey Robinson and the Miracles, the late great Gil Hodges, and the off-track bettors of America.

A poetry reading is about reading one's work, but again, as Gregory Corso had encouraged her, Patti is not just reading the words, she is infusing them with everything she can muster. She's setting a scene, she's engaging the audience, she's reading their energy and tailoring her performance to it. The nascent kinetics of that first reading in '71 had established itself as her signature style. Her presentation was animated and engaging, she was clearly modeling her rhythm and phrasing on rock and roll, and she executed it with enthusiastic verve. She was excited to be reading her work to an audience, and that feeling was tangible.

Her poems also appeared in what might have seemed like an unlikely location: *CREEM* magazine. The Detroit music magazine was known for being irreverent and anti-establishment, and while she did write some actual rock journalism for them, they also published her poetry because they could see the rock and roll and the energy in it. Their readers saw it, too, and they famously didn't like *anything*. As one wrote, "We don't need more like her, we need more of her."[21]

The response—positive or negative—to her work kept propelling Patti forward. She put together her own reading in honor of Jim Morrison at a downtown loft space, getting the word out with an ad in the *Village Voice* and fliers around downtown, and people showed up. This wasn't a captive crowd, there to see a headliner but forced to sit through the poetry; these were individuals tangibly responding to Patti's concepts and ideas, affirming to both Patti and Jane Friedman that there was an audience for her work. They talked about how to broaden her presentation, and Friedman encouraged her to bring Lenny Kaye—who had been in the crowd at the Morrison reading—back into the mix.

Patti's next self-produced concept was a series of readings under the umbrella "Rock n' Rimbaud," where she was joined by Lenny and occasionally other musicians. Again, her supporters, scenesters, and the just plain curious flocked to the event. "It occurred to me that, instead of this being a onetime event, we had the potential of something to build on," she remembered.[22] Friedman kept looking for more opportunities for the two to perform, getting Patti readings in bars when she could and bringing Lenny along when it worked. Toward the end of the year, they were rewarded for their diligence with an invitation to open for the political singer-songwriter Phil Ochs, playing two sets a night for six days at Max's Kansas City.

Patti and Lenny had been talking about adding a pianist, another step moving this still undefined but growing body of work forward. They spent a day auditioning keyboard players, hoping to find someone who wasn't just talented but would also fit into what they were building. "We thought a piano would suit our style, being both percussive and melodic," Patti said.[23] They found who they needed in Richard Sohl, whom Patti christened "DNV" because he physically resembled Tadzio, the main character in the 1971 film adaptation of Thomas Mann's novella *Death in Venice*.[24] Sohl was classically trained but that day demonstrated that he was comfortable with any style of music, and importantly, he played with the unfazed flexibility of a piano bar musician in a Bourbon Street bar on a Saturday night. He could follow Patti anywhere, and onstage he always watched her like a hawk, ready to pull back or fill a moment.

The future Patti Smith Group wasn't a piano-based band, but Sohl's musicianship and songwriting chops were critical to its sound. He added a warmth and fluidity that wasn't exactly what anyone expected to hear from a band that would be grouped into what would soon be called "punk rock." His musical contributions to Patti's body of work were bedrock; imagine "Free Money," "Frederick," or especially "Because the Night" without Sohl's deliberate, expressive introductions, "Birdland" without the mystical swirl he invoked, or the simple pathos of the piano in "The Jackson Song." His work was part of what made them transcend.

But on that March day in 1974, the curly-haired dude sent uptown on the recommendation of Danny Fields — the free-spirited music industry maven who handled PR for the Doors, signed both the MC5 and the Stooges to record contracts, and would shortly end up managing the Ramones—was a welcome addition to what Patti and Lenny were building. Patti's slogan "three chords merged with the power of the word" derived from the moment DNV joined the duo, a way to try to describe what they were doing, a way to differentiate it from anything else that was out there—or at least a way to warn the unsuspecting.

In the early 1970s, there simply were not that many places in New York City for an unsigned band playing original material. At that time, bands worked their way up from the Bottom Line to the Academy of Music to the Felt Forum to, finally, Madison Square Garden.[25] There were still folk clubs in the Village, left over from the 1960s, but they were mostly tourist traps. There was Max's Kansas City, but even there, a band needed a strong following or label support. The Mercer Arts Center literally collapsed into a pile of rubble in August 1973, which left a big void. Club 82, a former East Village bar for drag queens, opened its doors to glam rock, and the Coventry out in Sunnyside was also friendly to the star-spangled set—but it was *in Queens*.

A new band calling themselves Television organized and played their first show at a small theater in March 1974. But one venue does not a scene make, and it put the onus of the gig's promotion on the band and its manager. One day, Tom Verlaine and Richard Lloyd, both guitarists in the band, were walking down the Bowery and passed a bar. The proprietor was outside hanging his new awning. CBGB and OMFUG, it read, which the owner, Hilly Kristal, told them stood for Country Blue Grass and Blues and Other Music For Uplifting Gourmandizers. They convinced him to let them have Sunday nights, the quietest night of the week, and promised that he would make money on the bar if he let them have the door. They charged two dollars.

The first Television show at CB's, as the club would become known around the world, happened a few weeks later, on March 31. They continued to play every Sunday, telling their friends, coworkers, neighbors, and other like-minded comrades to come on down, regularly pulling in twenty to thirty people. Other bands soon approached Kristal and asked for a booking, like the Stilettos, featuring a guitar player named Chris Stein and a lead singer named Debbie Harry. The Stilettos would eventually become Blondie, the most commercially successful of all the punk bands. At the same time, four friends from Queens who called themselves the Ramones organized their own show at a loft space near Gramercy Park; they too would shortly find their way down to 315 Bowery.

If this all seems like some kind of magic, understand that the scenes were small, and once you found your people, you made a deliberate effort to stick together. "The people that were at Club 82—Lenny Kaye, Joey Ramone, Tommy Ramone... Gary Valentine, Debbie [Harry] and Chris [Stein], Johnny Thunders—essentially, everybody took their platforms off, cut their hair, walked around the corner, and wound up at CBGB," said Blondie drummer Clem Burke.[26] "It was the same 25 or 35 people in the audience," explained Lenny, "and you would get up onstage and play, and then go offstage and hang out and watch your friends play."[27]

If you've ever heard stories about what a dump CBGB was, they are all true. They were true when the place opened, and they were true in the early 1980s when I walked in the door with a fake ID at the age of sixteen. The room was long and narrow, with the bar along the right side, and at the time, the stage was along the left wall (it would later move to the back of the club). According to Alan Vega of Suicide, the experimental shock-rock duo who became part of the scene, "the bathrooms were already horrific, even before it was renamed CBGB."[28]

It was a forgotten bar in a part of town you avoided unless you had no other options, which made it the perfect place to inadvertently launch a revolution. The Bowery Mission was just down the road, and SRO (single room occupancy) hotels were everywhere, including right above the club. Unhoused people slept on the sidewalk, and in the winter, the street glowed with fires lit in trash barrels that the sleepers used to keep warm. (This is something I saw for myself as a kid when we drove down to Katz's Delicatessen to grab some pastrami to take back to Connecticut.) The location both protected it from noise complaints and ensured that the only people showing up wanted to be there; even in the 1980s, you planned your route to and from the club carefully so you didn't get jumped. But after Television planted their flag, it would only take about a year before limousines were pulling up in front of the club.

In April 1974, following the premiere of *Ladies and Gentlemen: The Rolling Stones*, Patti and Lenny made their way to the club on the Bowery at the invitation of Television's Richard Hell and Richard Lloyd. Hell knew Patti from the poetry scene; everyone knew Lenny Kaye because he wrote about music, worked in a record store, and had been showing up at the Mercer, Club 82, or anywhere else live music was happening. Lenny was particularly known to rock and roll aficionados because of his work putting together a compilation album called *Nuggets: Original Artyfacts from the First Psychedelic Era 1965–1968.*

Nuggets was a collection of amazing garage rock singles recorded in the mid-1960s that, by the early '70s, had virtually disappeared. Among the tracks were now-acknowledged classics such as "I Had Too Much to Dream (Last Night)" by the Electric Prunes, "Psychotic Reaction" by the Count Five, "Dirty Water" by the Standells, and "Pushin' Too Hard" by the Seeds, among many others. The compilation didn't sell that well on its initial release, but over time it turned into a cultural lodestone, where knowing the songs and bands that appeared on the record signified a shared ethos and common understanding of the important rudiments of rock and roll music. Hell and Verlaine knew the record before they knew the man behind it; countless others who would either step onto the stage or show up to watch the bands would also declare their allegiance to its fuzztone excellence.

Both Patti and Lenny were excited by Televison's performance as well as with the idea of the club as a place for bands like theirs to perform. A few months later, Television would open for Patti, Lenny, and Richard for half a dozen shows at Max's Kansas City; an allegiance had been formed. "We were working in the same outer limits" is how Lenny explained it.[29] And Television would be their chosen comrades when Patti would finally play CBGB in early 1975.

A few months later, the trio of Smith, Kaye, and Sohl entered Jimi Hendrix's Electric Lady Studios on West Eighth Street to make a record. In that era, while it wasn't unheard of for musicians to record and release their own material, it was unusual to enter a studio without record company support because it was expensive and required skill, two formidable barriers. But Lenny knew his way around a recording studio, and Robert Mapplethorpe offered to fund the project. It didn't seem all that foreign a concept to all involved because on the poetry scene poets were always putting out chapbooks, and this DIY — do it yourself — ethos would soon become fundamental to the burgeoning punk rock scene wherever it sprang up.

Making a record was also an incredibly smart and forward-thinking decision. "We wanted to see if we could get the magic we felt we were creating onstage onto a record," explained Lenny.[30] If the magic couldn't be captured on vinyl, it was a problem that would have to be resolved somehow. At the time, the path forward for unsigned musicians was to get signed to a record deal and then to make records. Better to find out early that adjustments need to be made and make them on your own time rather than fall flat and end up in the cut-out bin.[31]

A version of Hendrix's "Hey Joe" was meant as the A-side, with lyrics ripped out of the headlines: the kidnapping of the heiress Patty Hearst dominated the news cycle. The saga was terrifying and scintillating in equal amounts and inspired Patti to write what she called a "meditation on her situation."[32] The instrumentation was languid and yet dissonant, exactly what you would expect from the combination of musicians: Sohl's chords filled the space and fed both melody and rhythm, Lenny provided solidity and backbone, and Television's Tom Verlaine (whom they had asked to join for the session as a second guitarist) issued the aural equivalent of broken glass. And Patti sounds triumphant, ecstatic, like someone on the verge of a great adventure.

The B-side was "Piss Factory," Patti's poem set over music written by Richard Sohl. It was and remains a remarkable composition. Sohl constructed a melody that conveys tension and frustration as Patti relates the story of her escape from New Jersey, of breaking free from what could have been her destiny if she didn't hold fast to her belief in herself and get out. "Hey Joe" is gorgeous, but on "Piss Factory" she is so very much herself, exhibiting swagger, attitude, confidence, and truth:

> I will never return
> Never return
> No, never return to burn out at this Piss factory
> And I will travel light
> Oh, watch me now.[33]

It was breathtaking then and remains so right now.

The single was pressed and attributed to Mer Records ("Music of the most high," the label read, which with Lenny and Patti's love of reggae, was not false advertising). Jane Friedman sold copies for two dollars out of a shopping bag at the entrance to shows, and it ended up on the jukebox at Max's, a place of great honor. The musicians were surprised to learn that "Piss Factory" was more popular than "Hey Joe." They shouldn't have been, but it was yet another sign that things were moving in the right direction.

Back in New Jersey, another young musician at the start of his career found himself intrigued by a photograph of Patti in *CREEM*. "I was keeping an eye on the competition," Bruce Springsteen told me. "The first thing I heard was the song 'Piss Factory,' and so I said, 'Whoa, somebody else is writing about working people. Who's doing this right now?' Because there weren't that many people doing it."[34]

The trio headed out to the West Coast in November, playing at the infamous Whisky a Go Go on the Sunset Strip and then heading up to the Bay Area for a free show at a record store, a poetry reading, and an impromptu appearance at promoter Bill Graham's Winterland Ballroom. There was a tremendous response from the California kids, who have remained loyal to this day.

Theresa Kereakes, a teenage photographer who became a vital part of the LA punk scene, told me:

> There was a small group of us that read all the papers. We were aware of Patti, we were aware of the whole downtown New York scene, and very eagerly anticipated their presence on the West Coast, record deal or no. . . . We really looked up to New York, because as glam kids who were morphing into punk kids, this was like — these people knew the New York Dolls! They came up in the same petri dish — we just wanted to be a degree of separation from that.[35]

The California trip was incredibly validating to the band, but it also revealed their weaknesses. For the Winterland gig, they borrowed Allen Lanier, who played keyboards and guitar for Blue Öyster Cult and was Patti's main squeeze, as well as Jonathan Richman from Boston proto-punks the Modern Lovers on drums. "By then the music had grown to the point where we needed somebody else," remembered Lenny. "I was really trying to keep the rhythm going. I couldn't really do anything else."[36] But finding someone simpatico proved challenging because, in Patti's words, "none of them warmed up to the idea of a girl being the leader."[37]

In the end, the winner was Ivan Král, who had been a teenage rock star in his native Czechoslovakia until he and his family fled the country in 1966, a story he wrote about in the song "Citizen Ship" on *Wave* in 1979. He, too, had been hovering around the glam rock scene in a band called Luger before joining forces with Debbie Harry and Chris Stein in what became Blondie.

Ivan Král wasn't a flashy guitarist, but he was confident, competent, and malleable, which was exactly what Patti, Lenny, and Richard needed. "What we liked the most about him," Lenny explained, "we didn't have to change what we were doing; we sounded like ourselves, only bigger."[38] He could trade off on bass with Lenny and provide a reliable backing on rhythm guitar so that when the others meandered off into improvisation land, there was someone tethering them to the ground. He was a meat-and-potatoes classic rock kind of guy, and you can hear it in the songs he cowrote, like "Ain't It Strange," "25th Floor," and, most notably, "Dancing Barefoot," which would become one of Patti's most-covered songs. And you can hear it when he would take the spotlight, picking covers like Elvis's "Jailhouse Rock" or the Stones' "Time Is on My Side." (In 1976,

Rock Scene would breathlessly report, "Patti Smith and Ivan Král keep a photo of Keith on every hotel room wall they stay in."[39])

Ivan was in place in time for the band's first appearance at CBGB in February 1975, once again with Television in the support slot. Everyone in the band had been hanging out at the bar and going to shows, but it took the nascent PSG almost a year to get onstage there. But they made up for lost time: February, March, and April of that year was effectively a Patti Smith Group boot camp. They were booked into CB's for at least twenty-five nights running, with two shows per weeknight and three on weekends. And they filled the place; it put CBGB on the map at a time when no one else was selling out shows at the club on the weekend (or any other time, for that matter).

The genius and diligence of this approach is awe-inspiring. It gave the PSG the benefits of being on the road without having to *be on the road*. They got to work out their songs, build cohesiveness and momentum as a live act, find out what worked and—more importantly—what didn't, in front of a mostly sympathetic hometown crowd. Practicing in rehearsal spaces is necessary, but it can never replace playing in front of an audience. Any of the CB's bands could have taken this approach, and while there were other multi-night residencies, no one else was showing up with such intensity. Is it any wonder that they were the first band to get a major label deal? "We became a real band after that gig," said Lenny.[40]

Patti Smith came to New York City to work. Clive Davis took her at her word, and she signed a seven-record, $750,000 deal (worth about $3.75 million in 2021) with his new label, Arista Records, toward the end of March. The size and length of the contract indicated an investment; it wasn't what was known as an "artist development deal," an arrangement whereby a record company provides a modest financial outlay for an artist they think has promise, so the band can afford to buy some equipment or focus on songwriting instead of day jobs. This was the real thing.

The legend says that Patti, Lenny, DNV, and Ivan found their drummer, Jay Dee Daugherty, because he responded to a plea issued on a live radio appearance in May 1975 on WBAI's *Free Music Store* program: "We need a drummer and know you're out there."[41] The truth is a little more prosaic than that. Jay Dee had recently moved from California to New York with his friends in Lance Loud's band the Mumps, who had been pestering Television to let them open for them at CB's. "CBGB had no PA system. When I let Television know that I worked at a hi-fi store and could 'borrow' a cobbled-together sound system, we suddenly were in," Jay Dee explained. "I hung home stereo speakers (Bose 901s) from the ceiling, put a monitor speaker on top of the bar's awning pointed towards the erstwhile stage, and had a couple of mismatched microphones. It sounded great."[42] When Patti and Television were booked at CBGB for the February residency, Jane Friedman asked

Jay Dee if he could both provide sound for and record the performances.

"I was paid the princely sum of twenty-five dollars a show," he continued. "I'm sure I expressed my willingness to play with Patti to Jane, no doubt more than once. I had seen Patti at Max's Kansas City when it was just her, Lenny, and Richard DNV Sohl, and I was mesmerized; it was musical lust at first sight. So obvious that this was a band that was missing a drummer. So playing with her has been a dream come true ever since."[43]

Like Ivan, Jay Dee wasn't flashy; his style was crisp and reasonably disciplined enough that he hit the drums with precision and authority, but not so much that he couldn't ride the ebb and flow of an improvisation or tangent. His playing rounded out the songs and supercharged the live show. He created parts that you noticed: the martial roar of the tom-toms in "Till Victory," the intricacy of the fills on "Privilege," the majestic, heart-stopping roll into the chorus of "Because the Night," and the way he becomes the engine that drives Johnny in "Land," to name a few.

Jay Dee was in, but before the band went into the studio to record their first album for Arista, they arranged a gig to showcase their latest member, both for Clive Davis and anyone else in the scene. As it happened, Davis was not the only one dropping in to the Other End, a Village nightclub, to check things out that night; none other than Bob Dylan wandered in, sat down at the bar, and watched the set. This wasn't accidental; it was either the result of a nod from their mutual friend Bob Neuwirth or perhaps just the old guard checking out the vanguard. Patti clocked him in the room, and her already vivid energy soared.

According to James Wolcott of the *Village Voice*, "She was positively playing to Dylan."[44] He didn't mean that in a pejorative sense; this was the Bobby D. of 1975, fresh off *Blood on the Tracks*, full of charisma and mystery, and Wolcott points out that when Bob came backstage to introduce himself "everyone was excitedly unsettled."[45] Patti would later write about the evening, "It seemed for me a night of initiation, where I had to become fully myself in the presence of the one I had modeled myself after."[46]

For Patti, Dylan's presence was both a teenage fever dream and the ultimate validation. In 1993, she explained, "What had I derived from him and others like him, besides the ability to choose just the right dark glasses? The ability to fend for myself."[47] She didn't yet realize she would one day be in the position to extend that same gift to us.

In early September 1975, Patti, Lenny, and Richard headed back to Electric Lady, this time with their own guitarist and their brand-new drummer, to record *Horses*, their first album for Arista. John Cale, best known for his work in the Velvet Underground, the revolutionary rock and roll band that evolved out of Andy Warhol's Factory, was Patti's choice to produce the record. The Velvets were the spiritual godparents of everything that was happening at CBGB, and the band regularly covered their songs, namely

"Pale Blue Eyes" and "We're Gonna Have a Real Good Time Together."

This made him seem like the perfect fit for this project, but Patti, when asked about her experience working with him, described it as being "like A Season in Hell."[48] In another interview she elaborated, saying, tellingly, "All I was really looking for was a technical person. Instead, I got a total maniac artist."[49] Cale was always complimentary about his time working with Patti (and often showed up at gigs to sit in on bass), and Patti has since explained, "I didn't know what a producer did. I was suspicious, trying to guard my work."[50] I get it, though. When "What was it like to work with John Cale?" is the first question from a journalist in an interview about your first record, you want to keep the focus on yourself and your band and not let anyone plant seeds of doubt that anyone else might have been responsible for the quality of the end product.

But the end product was phenomenal, and John Cale was exactly the right person for this group of musicians at this moment in their career. He didn't make them sound like anyone except themselves and captured a specific, deliberate sensibility, an open, unadorned sound and overall vibe more accurately than any other working producer would have done. It wasn't even the "punk rock" label; if it was hard to find a guitar player who would take orders from a woman, it was going to be a million times harder to find a producer who would, given that most were part of a music business machine just as sexist and retrograde as every other industry.[51] Ultimately, Cale and Patti were at odds with each other because they were both stubborn motherfuckers acting in the highest service of the art, and the result was one of the best and most important albums in the history of rock and roll.

Horses as a body of work remains perfect. Any end-to-end listen even forty years later can still inspire awe. Some pieces of music are so utterly transformative that the opening salvo will forever remain a call to arms: the single snare drum shot that ushers in Bob Dylan's "Like a Rolling Stone," the majestic descending crescendo that opens Ike and Tina Turner's "River Deep, Mountain High," or the locomotive grunge roaring at the start of David Bowie's "Suffragette City" are just a few examples. The piano intro that pulls you into "Gloria," the opening track of *Horses*, is firmly on that list.

The measured, even piano chords are almost illusive, and then we hear Patti's voice making her declaration of artistic independence: "Jesus died for somebody's sins, but not mine." In that moment, it is just her, and Richard behind her, then small guitar tones, before the verbal and instrumental assertion:

> my sins my own
> they belong to me.
> Me.

On the first "me," her voice raises in volume, and on the second, it is louder, emphatic, declarative. The singer is speaking directly to us, and she wants to make sure we can hear her.

With the next verse, the rest of the musicians materialize and, with Patti, settle into a groove, still based on the E, A, D three-chord progression of the song's inspiration, Van Morrison and Them's classic "Gloria."[52] Patti's "Gloria" is kin to Morrison's. It is related by passion and attitude and a similar mysticism that swirls around the stories. But it is also very much *not* the same song. The original is seedy and dark; the reworked "Gloria" is ecstatic. The former is a pop single lasting two and a half minutes; the latter is a six-minute journey.

A woman is singing the song; she mentions seeing a "sweet young thing" outside on the parking meter. The first time you heard it and put those pieces together and then you listened to it again because you were not entirely sure what was going on: Is the narrator singing about herself? Is she singing about a man? In either case, she is singing about desire, and within the truly *glorious* bounds of this song, it does not matter, it is not something you have to figure out before you can feel the freedom and the elation being celebrated. You also understand Patti's assertions about being "beyond gender," which in 1975 was a statement both daring and brave because we are only a handful of years out from the Stonewall riots.

Halfway through we get to the chorus, which is wholesale lifted from Them's version, the recitation of the name — "G-L-O-R-I-A / Gloria" — a chorus rock and roll fans already know. The energy ratchets up and stays there, and then it pauses for the last verse when Patti reminds us, again, of her initial avowal, and you think it's over — except it's not. It's time for another joyful chorus on the fade-out.

"Redondo Beach" was the first time that Patti and Lenny's love of reggae would make its way into a song and onto a record. Reggae was still very much a new genre in the States, first coming onto music fans' radar via the soundtrack to the Jamaican crime film *The Harder They Come* in 1973. That said, "Redondo" isn't a reggae song, but a rock song strongly influenced by reggae, primarily through the distinctive offbeat rhythmic pattern. Lenny handled the upbeats on the guitar, while Ivan held down the bottom on bass. Patti sings the song not like a reggae singer (which would have been ridiculous) but instead just swings with the beat.

The song is written in three-line stanzas, and her adherence to that form adds to the compression that natively occurs in songs and poems. So she paints the scene in short, precise, almost impressionistic sketches, like "Late afternoon dreaming hotel" or "Sad description oh I was looking for you." It's almost a 1950s teenage tragedy song, and there's a bit of a girl group croon in Patti's voice.

His father died and left him a little farm in New England.

"Birdland" is a remarkable composition. The recording on *Horses* is an improvisation, recorded live in the studio. The spirit of improvisation is a vital part of the Patti Smith Group that doesn't get enough attention. I think some of it is because most people think of "improvisation" as something sloppy or haphazard that goes on for too long; they don't think of it as something that can present itself as a complex, fully realized song.

Lyrically, "Birdland" draws from UFOs, underwater birds, fathers and sons, John Coltrane, jazz, orphans, and other esoteric and not-so-esoteric subjects. Patti had a loose story, which would key off that first line, about a young boy losing his father and imagining that he would return on a spaceship to rescue him from this planet and take him away. Beyond that, it is also calling on the emotions of someone who doesn't feel like they fit in — "I'm not human" — and how many misfits are so desperate to escape their reality that they would welcome being abducted by aliens. The song also calls on Patti's stories about how just existing in her body in South Jersey engendered hostility and animosity because she wasn't like anybody else, and furthermore, she didn't *want* to be like anybody else. So she dreams of an escape of any kind.

Improvisation requires humility and trust and both the willingness and the ability to communicate. This means the individual musicians in the band must follow Patti wherever she goes, but also anticipate what she might do next, and respond to changes, surprises, or mistakes. "Birdland" is riveting; you hang on every word, willing her forward. It doesn't drag; she attenuates the energy through the pace and the flow of the vocals, which then in turn influence the instrumentation.

The chant at the end comes from an ancient rhythm and blues single by Huey "Piano" Smith (no relation), which chants, "We like birdland / we like birdland," over a rollicking piano melody, interspersed with a "sha da do wop da shaman do way" chorus. The record came out in 1958, and it feels like one of those oldies she remembered from her childhood.

"Birdland" is the first improvisation the band committed to record, but it wouldn't be the last. There has been a lengthy improv on almost every record she has released,[53] and this means there is always a moment in the live show where we go on that leap of faith with her. I had never read *A Book of Dreams*, the book that inspired "Birdland," until recently, and yet the image of the farm and the field and the trees and the long black limousines and the desperately sad young boy were always so clear to me in my mind (the spaceships not so much). Again, I attribute this to her precision in what details she reveals. In art, sometimes what is left out is more important than what is brought in.

The blithe, delicate chords that open "Free Money" are some of Richard Sohl's most evocative work; they feel cautiously hopeful as Patti sings, "Every night before I go to sleep / Find a ticket, win a lottery." The idea for the song came from her childhood and how every cent counted, and how her mother (who never actually bought a lottery ticket) would imagine that she had won and make lists of what she would do with the money. Patti's voice is elastic, emotive, and energetic, but you don't expect it to turn the corner into the brisk and joyful rocker that "Free Money" becomes. It's the opposite of "Birdland" in that it is tight and crisp, and it showcases a stellar performance from every single member of the band. The rolling drum crescendo in the bridge is particularly effective and reinforces the overall mood.

"Kimberly" is, at its core, a song about sisterly devotion. Kimberly is the name of Patti's youngest sister (and the other musician in the family), and the song as written is a ballad and a lullaby — one in which the stars descend from the universe, and Patti tries to both decode and illustrate childhood visions. The song is a deliberate dichotomy: the music is light and airy and not at all foreboding; lyrically, there's a lot to untangle, and the imagery is vivid. "And the sky split and the planets hit / Balls of jade dropped and existence stopped," Patti sings, while in other verses there are "bats with baby vein faces." The harmonies at the end sound like a group of kids standing on the corner under a streetlight, singing doo wop.

Although it was inspired by and written for Jim Morrison, "Break It Up" has the closest allegiance to Jimi Hendrix. This is because of the focused, exquisitely restrained guitar line written and performed by Tom Verlaine that forms the song's connective tissue. In accompaniment, Richard Sohl performs the most beautiful counterpart to Verlaine's work; it is simple, but he always manages to express so much emotion through his notes. But Verlaine's guitar line is simply astonishing. He is manifesting an aural embodiment of Hendrix's cosmology, and yet it is unmistakably his (which is, of course, a thing I say in hindsight because the first Television single hadn't even been recorded yet).

Lyrically, it was a dream and a myth, and I also think a way of trying to make sense of why so many of the artists who were walking the edges of the mainstream and were of personal significance to Patti had died. The lyrics tell the story of her coming upon Jim Morrison alive but bound to earth with wings made of marble. If she can pray long enough, she could free him. She couldn't save Morrison (or Hendrix or Joplin or Brian Jones), but here in her dream she could at least help him escape this mortal plane.

Patti and Richard are alone on the verses of the song, but the rest of the band comes in on the choruses; she declares the action—"he cried / he sang / I cried"—and they shout in response, "Break it up!" On the last verse, Patti literally pounds her chest, using the percussion the motion produces as another instrument. This is the section where the narrator is now trying to break out of their own skin; he/she/they succeed by the song's end.

*   *   *

"Land," up next, is deliberately written as a trilogy. While "Oath" is the genesis of *Horses*, "Land" is the molten core, the ne plus ultra.

The boy was in the hallway drinking a glass of tea

Patti's voice is low but matter of fact. Almost conversational.

From the other end of the hallway a rhythm was generating.

Now there's a little bit of echo, the track shifts from channel to channel quickly, and you hear the rhythm on the guitar, dissonant. Then everything ramps up, and you feel the violence in the lyrics, both in the voice and the tone. It is menace; Johnny is being violated. It is over in a flash, and we don't know whether Johnny is alive or dead — the first few times I heard the song I thought he had been stabbed — but then, the clarion call:

he's being surrounded by
horses horses horses horses.

They are imaginary friends, guardians, protectors, angels. We know this because after Patti chants to invoke the spirits, she shifts into another kind of invocation, the opening of "Land of a Thousand Dances," which asks the eternal question: "Do you know how to pony?" The original song was written by New Orleans' own Chris Kenner, but the version Patti probably knew best was the one by R & B great Wilson Pickett. Kenner's inspiration came from a gospel song; Patti's inspiration came from AM radio, William Burroughs's *The Wild Boys*, and a hot restless city full of abandon. There were never a thousand dances in the original song. It was about the freedom of movement, the rebellion of new dances that scandalize older generations, the heat and energy of youth, and so is Patti's version.

"La Mer (de)" is the third scene. It is the comedown or, perhaps, the bardo, the intermediate state. The music deconstructs, breaks down; Patti's voice is quiet, almost a whisper, paper thin. The joke in the title is both a reference to the refrain in this passage about the "sea of possibilities" and, of course, the French word for shit. Her voice softly fades out; the drums beat, skip a beat, heartbeat, end.

The ten minutes of "Land" has its defined pieces, but it is also wide and free-ranging in its own way, with "La Mer (de)" sometimes veering off course into, well, the *sea of possibilities*. It is truly an ensemble piece in that everyone in the band plays a critical role — the rock band must rock and roll. Richard's colorations are particularly rich. But they all need to shift seamlessly from recitation to dance party to psychedelic free-float. And this isn't something manufactured on tape, but rather an accurate capture of what the band could do live.

"Elegie" is the end, and it is primarily meant as an homage to Hendrix, but is also a tribute to fallen friends.

Allen Lanier wrote the song with Patti, and he plays the bluesy guitar riffs that percolate through the song. It is a simple arrangement (bass, vocals, guitar, and piano), with Richard's melody dominating. Patti's voice is deep and rich, with a slight tinge of formality befitting the subject matter.

On the last night of CBGB in 2006, the band performed "Elegie," and Patti pulled out a piece of paper and began reading a list of names, those in the tribe that formed in that place whom we lost over the decades. It was a beautiful tribute to fallen friends and a vehicle of public mourning for both the individuals and the ground on which we all stood.

The way she can distill emotion, the way she selects elements of a dream or a vision or a concept to include in a song or a poem — it is as Mapplethorpe always told her, "Nobody sees like we do," and nobody did or has managed to duplicate or eclipse her. What she has inspired is what she had always wanted, people who took inspiration from her and then made their own art.

Patti's contract with Arista afforded her complete artistic control, which included her album covers. "There was never any question that Robert would take the portrait for the cover of *Horses*," she stated in *Just Kids*.[54] And thanks to that book, we know the behind-the-scenes details of the collaboration that produced it. Robert watching the sun and the shadow move across the wall of Sam Wagstaff's apartment and realizing what he wanted to do. Patti choosing the white button-down shirt, the black pants, the black ribbon in honor of Baudelaire hanging from her neck and tucked under the collar. The suit jacket, slung over the shoulder with perfect attitude and nonchalance in a nod to fellow New Jerseyan Frank Sinatra. On the lapel, the tiny sterling silver pin of a horse in mid-stride, a gift from Allen Lanier. The hairstyle, that homage to Keith Richards.

The cover of *Horses* was as much a statement of intent as the music inside: a woman with no makeup, messy hair, a man's shirt, a man's tie, a man's jacket, shot in a black and white that was as stark as it was stunning. Patti stands in a posture of complete assurance and self-confidence, facing the camera, and the audience, with an expression of perfect equanimity. She is not smiling, she is not selling, she is just there, with that bar of sunlight and its accompanying shadow as the only adornment. Her outfit, and her expression, said that she did not care what anyone thought. It said that she didn't fit in and she had stopped trying a long time ago. It said that she was comfortable where she was. It was the uniform of the kind of outsider whose very existence in the world irked the members of the status quo. She was our pathfinder; she had already walked down the trail and left signs: feathers, stone cairns, sticks laid out in particular patterns, blazes affixed to the trees.

Horses was a signal to the rest of us that there was a way out.

Horses hit record stores shelves on Monday, November 10, 1975, just in time for Christmas sales. The record charted on the *Billboard* 200, where it stayed for seventeen weeks and reached number 47. You know that someone, somewhere, likely in a bar south of Fourteenth Street in Manhattan, muttered something about how caring about *Billboard* and charts was *selling out to the man* and *not very punk rock*, but is there anything honestly more punk rock than breaking into the enemy's fortress and walking around like you belong? It mattered because it was a seven-album deal, because she was an early signing to Clive Davis's new record label, and because her success would mean other labels would be willing to take a chance on other downtown bands. It was a big fucking deal, actually.

The album garnered sufficient notice, with not one but three pieces — a review, a profile, and a piece on up-and-coming artists — in the *New York Times*. The profile in the Sunday magazine was written not by an arts critic but rather by two culture writers, who produced an article that has perhaps more distance or remove than would have come from someone closer to her work. I did not read this article when it came out but later found it in the library, and I was grateful I had not been a vocal supporter at the time because this is the piece where she first talked about her writing methodology: "I'd sit at the typewriter and type until I felt sexy, then I'd go and masturbate to get high, and then I'd come back in that higher place and write some more."[55] I would not have wanted to have had that conversation with my parents at that age (or any age, really) or be held publicly accountable for *that thing* that the person I liked had said.

Other journalists weighed in favorably on the album as well. Out in Detroit, Lester Bangs from *CREEM* issued a measured burst of deep approval, Robert Christgau gave her an A minus, and Greil Marcus, writing in the *Village Voice*, was disapproving but mostly positive. John Rockwell, an early and fervent supporter, reviewed the record for both the *New York Times* and *Rolling Stone*. Robert Hilburn gave the record a positive nod in the *Los Angeles Times*.

Patti's biggest supporters were still mostly within the alternative press and the growing fanzine culture. She also had a staunch ally in Lisa Robinson, a music writer who didn't consider herself to be a rock critic, maintaining, "I wrote gossippy columns and conducted interviews."[56] But Robinson consistently demonstrated a deep insight into what Patti was trying to do, and her reports and interviews reflect that.

Horses and Patti as an artist were warmly received by the UK music press in a way that was far less sexist and condescending than even the US journalists who *liked* her. Their reportage was also more egalitarian, seeing themselves on her same level and not like they were gurus on high deigning to consider her existence.

The January 1, 1976, issue of *Rolling Stone* weighed in with a significant story by Dave Marsh.[57] It was a good match not just because Marsh liked her music, but also because, as a fellow working-class kid, he could both relate to her influences and ambition while completely recognizing where she came from and what that ultimately meant. He lets her bullshit him, but within reason. It's also a solid summary of who she was and how she got to where she is. *Rolling Stone* was still counterculture at the time, but just establishment enough to count. More important, you could buy *Rolling Stone* in Chicago, Denver, Topeka, or Columbus. Her making it into the magazine opened up a place for the rest of downtown.

— 2 —

C'MON, GOD, MAKE A MOVE

It was almost midnight on a Saturday night in 1976 and I was sitting on the floor of my family's TV room, as close to the set as I could get without being chided for being too close, but close enough to allow for sufficient volume without being yelled at to turn it down. I was watching NBC's *Saturday Night Live*. I was a fairly sheltered, suburban twelve-year-old, so I didn't get most of the sketches, but my primary reason for watching was the musical acts. I do not remember ever not having insomnia and staying up later than I should, reading or listening to the radio; my mother also liked to stay up late, smoking, reading magazines, and watching old movies, and I would often sit up with her on weekends.

This night, however, the television was mine. The episode was hosted by White House press secretary Ron Nessen and featured filmed cameos of President Gerald Ford. And then, there it was, on the screen: PATTI SMITH GROUP. I don't know what I was expecting, but it floored me. There was a woman onstage and she was out front and it was her band: the musicians were supporting *her*.

She was wearing a white button-down shirt just like on the cover of *Horses* and an actual tie around her neck. Her hair was perfect, a jagged, black-hennaed mess. She didn't move around much—the stage was so small that Richard Sohl wasn't in any of the shots beyond the intro chords to "Gloria"[1]—but she was like one of those toys you would wind up and then let go and watch it spin. At the end of the song, before the last chorus, she was breathing hard, but she was smiling, she knew she done good. She murmured at the end "Happy Easter, CBGB." I knew what CBGB was because when my father would go into the city for business, he would come back with a record I had asked for or a magazine that had someone holding a guitar on the cover. One day he came home with *Rock Scene*. "I thought this was one of your bands," he said, pointing at David Bowie or Keith Richards.

That Monday, *Saturday Night Live* was a topic of conversation at school like it always was. Except that I did not completely understand that being a fan of this band, a band that no one else had written on their blue canvas three-ring notebook except me, meant that I was now guilty by association. I was already "different": I didn't drink, smoke, or take drugs. Boys did not know I was alive. I liked to read and was always either juggling a stack of books or trying to hide behind one so I wouldn't be noticed. I didn't have many friends, and the friends I did have weren't music fans, at least not like I was. The other kids who were music fans wore Aerosmith T-shirts or carried around Jethro Tull or

Lynyrd Skynyrd albums.[2] I knew all that music because that was what you heard on FM radio, but it didn't mean that I liked it. I tried.

But this day was different because Patti had dared to step into their world. What fascinated and drew me in repelled others, and to them, their aversion was my fault. Patti hadn't gone onstage to be consumed; she didn't smile; she wasn't wearing a dress or even fancy stage clothes. I knew that she was Different, but she was just on national television. "Les . . . be . . . friends!" one of the popular kids yelled as I walked by; everyone else snickered or pretended to, so they wouldn't be a target. My head was down and I was looking at the floor, so I didn't see when someone walked by and bumped into me so I crashed into a locker. This was a town forty-five minutes away from New York City by train, but the message was clear: people like her — people like you who like her — are not welcome here. (As though I hadn't figured that out already.)

I think of an article about Patti in *Mademoiselle* in 1975, where she referred to the interview as "a revenge for bad skin," revenge on anyone back then who thought or called her weird.[3] In that same interview, she described the people she left behind in South Jersey: "They don't realize that all you have to do is get on the fucking train and you're in New York. In New York, all you have to do is get on a plane and you're in Paris."[4] The town my family lived in was exponentially closer to the city than Patti's town and was located in one of the richest counties in the country at the time, and yet somehow I was also surrounded by people with similarly small vistas.

But here she was: tangible proof that you could survive, you could get out, and you could *flourish*. "And I will travel light / oh, watch me now," she declared in "Piss Factory," and she was right.

In August, Patti and the band went back into the studio, this time with Jack Douglas as producer, to make their second album, *Radio Ethiopia*. Douglas's big credits at the time were Aerosmith and Cheap Trick, and he was known for making dense, bright, loud albums that sounded great on FM radio. It wasn't that *Horses* was unsuccessful, but there must have been a feeling that it wasn't successful *enough* that governed Patti's decision to choose someone so mainstream as producer. But the band was walking into the Record Plant with a robust set of material, all of which had been road-tested in varying degrees, so things were aligned to go well.

Everyone in the band cowrote songs with Patti, and it's easy to pick out Ivan's contributions: the big rock songs such as "Ask the Angels" or "Pumping (My Heart)" (to which Jay Dee also contributed). "Angels" is just an absolute delight. It is bright and soaring and Patti's voice sounds phenomenal, rich and full-throated. "Pumping (My Heart)" is a straight-ahead rocker with evocative, impressionistic lyrics that seem to describe how Patti felt onstage: "Baby gotta box in the center of the ring / And my heart starts pumping my fists start jumping," she sings, while the music conveys the urgency of "total abandon!" that the chorus declares.

"Ain't It Strange," with its dark and mystical scenes, is one of Patti Smith's best songs. She used to like to tell stories about Scheherazade onstage, pulling from her childhood love of *Arabian Nights*, and here she is telling a story about the hidden, the sacred, the secret, but she is also inhabiting a character. It brings in Eastern mysticism: "Hand of God I start to whirl" is right out of Rumi and the whirling dervishes. Then there is a one-drop on the rhythm, Richard levitates on organ, Lenny sings harmonies, and Ivan's guitar solo feels like a dry desert wind, a scirocco, blowing through the palace. It is meant to be dangerous and seductive, and it succeeds. I'm amazed when it appears in current setlists because it still maintains all its essential elements and in many ways is more powerful now.

"Pissing in a River" is at the other end of the emotional spectrum; it's a cross between a power ballad and a torch song, and Richard gets the MVP award for the light and space he creates on the piano and organ. The song's climax, after the guitar solo, is vivid and unexpected, and Patti just pours herself into it, making you feel the desperation, sadness, and loss: "What about it you're going to leave me / What about it I can't live without you." The anguish is palpable; live, it gets me in the center of my chest every single time.

In a world in which people either love or hate "Radio Ethiopia / Abyssinia," I am in the former camp, for a variety of reasons: because I never got to see it live, because it is dense and vivid, and because watching the Patti Smith Group join together in improvisation is a righteous thing to witness. Patti makes me believe that she is channeling the mojo of Rimbaud as he lay dying and dreaming of Abyssinia.

Most of all, I adore that she played guitar on it. Patti had bought an electric guitar, her Fender Duo-Sonic, which she would refer to as her weapon. (She also bought a Marshall amp.) As she told a journalist, "I don't just play guitar to 'melt into the soul' of Jimi Hendrix but to show that if a puny dumb girl from New Jersey can take this electric guitar and make it into a weapon then any kid can do it."[5] It was a few years later that I would walk down to West Forty-Eighth Street and buy myself a black Fender Strat from Manny's Music. I did not know how to play guitar, but I was going to try. Patti made me feel like I had every right to walk into the same store where Pete Townshend or Keith Richards bought their instruments, point to one on the wall, and claim it as my own.

I don't like "Poppies." As a teenager, I listened to the lyrics about taking heroin and how it felt. The song was more effective than any antidrug propaganda. (Even though my main reason for avoiding drugs was so I could get the hell out of my hometown. Then I could do drugs.) The music is also the least inventive on the album. In the days of record albums, it was inconvenient to skip over because it was the third song on side A, yet I always wanted to skip it because it set me on edge.

My complaint with *Radio Ethiopia* has always been with its production. Jack Douglas compressed the life out of Patti's voice and completely neutered the elastic energy she and the band had developed and then manifested on *Horses*. The production feels formulaic, as though the producer did not understand Patti's music and just passed the tape through some radio-friendly-unit-shifter filter and shrugged. There is no other explanation for what he did to some of the songs.

Radio Ethiopia did not meet with commercial success. But nothing in this album calls for the outrage that accompanied its release or the vitriol that continued for decades. This isn't just a record people dislike, it's a record that is widely reviled, sometimes violently so, with most of the complaints aimed at the production (agreed) and the rest at the title track. In the *New Musical Express*, Charles Shaar Murray referred to "Radio Ethiopia" in turn as "pretentious," "self-indulgent," and "inexcusable."[6] Robert Christgau noted in the *Village Voice* that Patti was "caught in a classic double-bind: accused of selling out by her former allies and of not selling by her new ones."[7]

Over the years, Lenny Kaye has defended the album by saying that it "wasn't an album of songs. It was an album of fields."[8] I don't think that's fair to the songs, but I believe he's trying to point out that its detractors didn't get what Patti and the band were trying to do. Both Patti and Lenny have continued to be proud of the record as an accomplishment and to defend it any time a journalist tries to bring it up as a failure or as the low point of her career.

Constantin Brancusi, the Romanian sculptor, is repeatedly referenced in "Radio Ethiopia," with specific mention of his sculpture *Bird in Space* and a suggestion that sculptors would be trading in their tools for electric guitars. *Bird in Space* is famous largely because when it was shipped to the United States to appear in an exhibition, US Customs refused to recognize it as a piece of art and charged duty against it as a "utilitarian object."[9] Brancusi took the matter to court and prevailed, with the judge deciding that the definition of art being used to evaluate the sculpture was out of date.

Patti Smith does nothing by accident.

Of course, the only reason I know about Brancusi is because Patti talks about him in the song and he went on my list of people to look up. I went to the library one day, pulled out an art book, and spent an afternoon looking at sculpture. I then knew who Brancusi was and why he was important. I meditated on that fact while viewing his retrospective at the Museum of Modern Art in 2016. I was at the exhibit because I had a membership to MoMA, and I had a membership to MoMA because when I had a couple of hours between classes in college, I would walk over to the museum to look at the Pollacks or Picassos or even just go into the bookstore and leaf through the photography books. That wasn't *just* because of Patti Smith, but she was a large part of why I became an adult who felt that art museums were fun and interesting rather than weird or boring.

In January 1977, the Patti Smith Group set out on their first arena tour, opening for Bob Seger and the Silver Bullet Band. If that sounds like a terrible mismatch, that's because it was. The music industry standards for pairing a promising up-and-coming band with a successful headliner is a good idea in theory but rarely plays out that way, as most music fans aren't that open-minded even when the pairing has more in common than this train wreck.[10] That isn't the reason that Patti fell off the stage during a show in Tampa, Florida, and landed on the concrete hockey arena floor fifteen feet below, but the unfriendly atmosphere certainly didn't help.

It was during "Ain't It Strange," where Patti would execute some of the whirling and spinning referenced in the song's lyrics. She sang, "C'mon, God, make a move," she spun, lost her balance, and fell. By some miracle, she did not break her neck; still, she sustained two cracked vertebrae and broken bones in her face and required twenty-two stitches to close the wounds on her head.

The accident obviously meant that the tour with Bob Seger was canceled, but also that any plans to be on the road promoting *Radio Ethiopia* were over. This was not great news for a record that was having a tough time gaining any commercial or critical foothold, but more importantly, Patti wasn't paralyzed and her prognosis for recovery was positive. She rejected the initial recommendation for surgery, opting for a course of intense physical therapy. Pictures of her wearing her neck brace while working out on a then new-fangled Nautilus machine appeared in *Rolling Stone* and *Rock Scene*.

She spent her recovery time working on *Babel*, her first major book of poetry; writing songs for her next record; and receiving a steady stream of visitors, well-wishers, and ne'er-do-wells to her apartment in Greenwich Village. The recuperating patient insisted to everyone that she would be back onstage by Easter, which, coincidentally, was also going to be the name of the next album.

The publication of *Babel* was significant because it was published by a mainstream house, G. P. Putnam's, which meant that you could walk into your mall bookstore and easily order it. I bought mine at the old Barnes & Noble on Fifth Avenue that was a stop on every family trip into Manhattan. Every issue of Patti's fan club newsletter (titled *de l'ame pour l'ame*, or "soul to soul," the dedication she gave Jane Friedman on *Horses*) listed the address of Gotham Book Mart so that fans could order copies of her chapbooks and other slim volumes.

I didn't understand much of *Babel*, but I kept reading it and rereading it because it was Patti's work and because I wanted to learn from her. I wasn't sure exactly what I wanted to learn, but I knew I wanted to be independent and strong and free and alive. I knew I wanted to be a writer, and she was the only role model I could see my-self in, someone who seemed to live in a brilliant, vivid, and interesting world. I read other poets—I liked Emily Dickinson and e. e. cummings and I owned a copy of Allen Ginsberg's *Howl*—and if a musician I liked mentioned a writer, I would go look for them in the library and read one book (or at least try to read it).

Poetry felt like a special language that if I could decode I would know more about the world. I wrote very bad poems, and I wish I had written more at the time; I wish I hadn't been trying for perfection or writing something that could be published in the school's literary magazine. I liked the pictures I could see in my head when I read poetry. When I moved to New York City to go to college, which was a year or two after Patti had moved to Detroit, I walked into the sanctuary at St. Mark's Church for a poetry reading as soon as possible. I imagined Patti standing there and reading. I went to poetry readings all the time as a normal, fun thing to do, even though most of the time I was going by myself because I hadn't met anyone yet who also thought that po-etry readings were awesome.

I am super grateful now for all the time I spent riding the D train alone, between my college in the Bronx and downtown Manhattan, because I got to see poets like Anne Waldman and John Giorno, Ginsberg at least once, and Jim Carroll so often that he knew me by sight and would always say hello and was always happy to talk to me about his band or his record or his last performance.

I didn't want to be a poet; I just wanted to live in a world that was filled with things that made me feel like part of something larger than the stupid, status-filled, consumerist, mall-visiting garbage I had grown up with in Fairfield County, Connecticut.

Poetry was a thing I had to stand up for. Poetry was a thing that would make other people angry. Poetry always reminded me of who I was, and who I wasn't. It was something to hang onto, along with art and rock and roll and books. Sometimes I needed it more than others, but I never sold my poetry books and they crossed continents and oceans with me. I still have my copy of *Babel*, which sits on my desk as I write this.

"BASIC TRAINING" read the top of the CBGB ads above the slot listing the dates Patti would appear in her return to the club in spring 1977. "Out of traction / back in action" read the slogan on the band's fliers, scrawled in thick black ink in Patti's distinctive handwriting. It was another CB's bootcamp, nine shows, running from May 31 to June 8. Patti wore her neck brace onstage for the first few nights, and reviews noted that she was understandably less physical in her onstage movements. There are, remarkably, bootleg recordings of five of the nine shows. They do not possess what anyone would term great fidelity, but it's enough to get the general vibe and to confirm the glowing press accolades from stalwarts like John Rockwell from the *New York Times*, who noted that she "moved like a gingerly stork in her neck brace."[11] But this was still energetically the very same Patti Smith, down to her banter with the audience and her enthusiastic endorsements for Flintstones vitamins.

The band entered the studio in August to record the next album. This time, the producer would be, like the PSG themselves, someone new to the business: a young Brooklynite named Jimmy Iovine, who had worked his way up through the NYC studio system as an engineer and mixer. Iovine wouldn't try to impose his artistic vision on the album, as John Cale had, nor did he have an established "sound," but like Jack Douglas, he had the technical chops behind the board that Patti needed. She had watched him working as an engineer with both John Lennon (*Walls and Bridges*) and Bruce Springsteen (*Born to Run* and *Darkness on the Edge of Town*), and although he hadn't yet sat in the producer's chair, she trusted him.

"To me, he did all the work," Smith told *Billboard* in 2018. "I like workers, and Jimmy was a worker. He would work twelve hours. I thought, 'This is the kind of person I want to work with. I don't want to work with someone of high standing who was a band psychologist or anything, or even a person with vision.' I wanted to work with a fellow worker."[12] It was this particular brand of hustle that resulted in Iovine's biggest contribution to the album.

Going into the recording sessions for *Easter*, Patti already had "Space Monkey," her rewrite of "Privilege (Set Me

Free)," and "Rock N Roll N———r" (hereafter "RnRN")[13] along with its spoken-word prelude, "Babelogue," recorded live at one of the CBGB "Basic Training" nights. In the pre-CD years, albums were twenty-two minutes a side, which for most artists equaled about five songs, so she was already halfway there. The other songs were coming together, and Patti and Lenny Kaye felt strongly that either "Till Victory" or "RnRN" should be the album's lead-off single, the selection sent out into the world to signal what the record was about. Jimmy Iovine disagreed, insisting, "We didn't have a single to get you into the album."[14]

Today, Iovine is known as a legendary producer and music industry mogul who founded Interscope Records and cofounded Beats Electronics with the hip-hop pioneer Dr. Dre. But in 1977, Iovine was a scrappy engineer in his mid-twenties who was currently engineering sessions for Bruce Springsteen that would become *Darkness on the Edge of Town*.

Following *Radio Ethiopia*'s lack of success, Arista Records would have strongly preferred that Patti hire someone with more of a production track record. "So I fought for Jimmy, and he had something to prove," Patti said. "Jimmy worked really hard with us, but he really wanted to make a special mark on this record."[15] Springsteen had a backlog of material for his record and was continuing to write, so he had a lot of unfinished songs lying around. This included a track initially called "The Night Belongs to Lovers."

As it happened, this was the first song Springsteen recorded on his first day in the studio, but he only had a rough vocal and no lyrics except the chorus. As Bruce moved his record in a different direction, Iovine zeroed in on the song. The details of when and where Iovine got Springsteen's blessing to walk that Maxell C46 cassette out of the studio differ slightly each time either of them tells the story, but it boils down to Iovine campaigning Springsteen for the song, and Bruce saying yes.[16]

Springsteen told me, "I was a tremendous admirer of Patti, you know, and I was just flattered that she was interested in collaborating, and I was just happy that she found something that she could do with the song, you know, because that song would still be in my archives, if it wasn't for her. And it would be something that nobody had ever heard of."[17]

There was one big problem: Patti was not interested in singing someone else's songs. She felt strongly about wanting to write and record her own material, whether by herself or with someone in the PSG. So the tape went home and sat on her mantel. "Even now it makes me laugh," Patti explained in 2017. "Every day I'd come to the studio, he [Iovine] wouldn't say hello to me, he'd say, 'Did you listen to the song? Did you listen to the song?' I'd say, 'No, I haven't listened to it yet.' 'Should we go back to your apartment and listen to the song?' For *days*. 'Did you listen to the song?'"

She continued:

> At that time, I was building a romance with my future husband, Fred "Sonic" Smith, and he lived in Detroit, so I only got to talk to him once a week. I'm home and I'm waiting for Fred to call. 7:30 comes, he doesn't call. 8:00 o'clock, I was getting really agitated, and I noticed the tape sitting on the mantle and I thought, "I'll listen to that darn song." I put it on and — it's flawlessly produced, great chorus, it's in my key, it's anthemic. So Fred finally calls me at like almost midnight, but by midnight, I'd written all the lyrics.[18]

The next day, Patti had a different answer when Iovine asked, "Did you listen to the song?" They recorded and finished it in two days.

The song, now titled "Because the Night," was released as a single right as *Easter* hit the streets and spent three months on the *Billboard* Hot 100, reaching number 13. In the United Kingdom, the single went to number 5 and was certified silver by the British Phonographic Industry, which means it sold more than 250,000 copies.[19] I asked Springsteen whether he remembered the first time he heard the song on the radio and whether he had any regrets. "I was just happy because I realized I had written a great chorus — that, I knew," he said. "But I didn't have the rest of the song! I had me mumbling kind of a few things and had a great hook, I knew that.... A great hook, as great as one can be, is still not a great song. And so she turned it into a great song."[20]

"Bruce wrote the music, and I always think of myself as the translator," Patti told an interviewer in 1978. "He gave me the music, and it had some mumbling on it, and Bruce is a genius mumbler, like the sexiest mumbler I ever heard.... He wrote the tag 'Because the night belongs to lovers,' which was in between the mumbling.... I respected his lyrics, and I thought it was a very nice sentiment, so I built the rest of the lyrics, which are obviously mine, around his sentiment."[21]

Springsteen continued, "Was I expecting for it to go to the top five, or whatever it did? Well, as far as I knew, none of us were doing that. I wasn't having any big hits, you know. [He laughs.] So it was a surprise when the record kind of actually cracked mainstream Top 40 radio. It was a surprise just because of the type of artist that Patti was also—but when it works, it works!"[22]

There was some rockist partisanship at the time of the single's release, with detractors muttering that Smith didn't actually *do* anything, that it was Bruce's song, and others once again charging that she had "sold out." The best response to that is her own: "Punk rock is about freedom, it's not about your chart position. And I'll sing any song I fucking want."[23]

"Because the Night" was made for FM radio, but it also stood out amid its competition. Patti's performance of the song embodied an intense vulnerability and yearning, and the emotional delivery of the lyrics was frank and unapologetic. Nowadays someone would probably call it "fierce," but reaching for an easy and overused label is a way of minimizing a woman taking up space and could not be further from the intent of the song. "Because the Night" was a grown woman singing about her wants and dreams, and there are no more perfect couplets than "love is a ring / the telephone" no matter the decade in which you listen to it. How do those six words manage to perfectly encompass that feeling of elation and relief when the phone finally rings and the right person is on the other end of it?

There was no way to know how this song would expand to fill the space it was given, that there would be a new cover of it in every generation, that it would fly out over the rooftops and become an anchor for the people who needed to hear it. In 2010, at the Rock & Roll Hall of Fame Twenty-Fifth Anniversary Concerts at Madison Square Garden, Bono introduced the song by saying that "this is the song we wish we'd written" before inviting both Bruce and Patti out to perform it with U2. As Lenny Kaye said, "I don't think that either Bruce or Patti understood the power of that song until it became a song and started riding up the charts. . . . And together we all made something that was greater than all of us."[24]

Easter was commercially successful (Patti prefers to say it was "communicative")[25] not just because of the hit single but also because it was an undeniably solid and thoroughly accessible record, showcasing the Patti Smith Group doing the things they did best, accompanied by production that was compatible with the material. Iovine *got* Patti and the band at an elemental level. Much as John Cale did on *Horses*, Iovine captured the musicians the way they were but gave them an aural polish that elevated the material yet still felt organic. The songs would sound good on the radio, but they would still sound like the Patti Smith Group.

There is so much to adore on *Easter*: the martial attention of "Till Victory," the cosmology in "Space Monkey," the otherworldly beauty of "Ghost Dance," the white hot rage in "25th Floor," the magnetic *snap* of "Babelogue" into "RnRN," recorded live so that you could get the feeling of what it was like to see the band onstage even if you never had the chance. There isn't a bad song on the record, and the band plays the heck out of each and every one (although to be fair, there isn't a Patti Smith record that exists where it feels like effort was lacking).

"Till Victory" should have opened or closed every concert since forever; it is exactly as triumphant and joyous as the title commands. Patti's voice has found its power; she is projecting, not shouting, which gives her tone a delightful resonance that extends throughout the record. It is a declaration of meaning and intent.

"Space Monkey" manages to be both esoteric and metaphysical (with a dash of ufology for good measure) but lyrically just slightly more direct and melodically more compact and accessible. If you're going to sing about seeing spaceships hovering over Ninth Avenue, make it easy for the listeners to come on that trip with you. Patti's voice is more rough-edged, but the delivery sounds smoother and less forced while still modulating between tones and emotions. Richard Sohl is absent from this record due to illness, but he makes an appearance on this track. Although his replacement, Bruce Brody from John Cale's band, is a strong player, he doesn't have the same sense of soul and lift that Richard did, and you can feel the difference here.

An element of Patti's albums I don't think gets enough attention is how beautifully sequenced they are. The emotional downshift from "Because the Night" into "Ghost Dance" (and then back up into "Babelogue") is perfectly executed: sonically and emotionally, the serenity of "Ghost Dance" isn't discordant after the giant pop single, and it gives listeners a moment to catch their breath. It is also just a flat-out gorgeous song, Patti sounding plaintive and prayerful, the band singing "We shall live again" behind her as its own instrument. You could sing it around a campfire. In the 1980s, when Lenny played with his own band, he would often sing "Ghost Dance" (which he cowrote), accompanying himself on acoustic guitar, and he always conveyed a little piece of the same soul. I loved going to see his band and felt I was lucky to get a bit of that magic.

"Privilege (Set Me Free)" is Patti's rewrite of a song from the 1967 British film, *Privilege*, about a pop star who rises to the top and how that influence and success can be seized and weaponized. There were also some deliberate messianic overtones, just the kind of thing that would pique Patti's interest. The film, which starred "It Girl" Jean Shrimpton and Paul Jones from Manfred Mann, is the kind of quintessential '60s Swinging London movie that would appeal to someone who had a love for the British Invasion (and Shrimpton had her place in Patti's pantheon of icons, much like Warhol superstar Edie Sedgwick).

The original is a stylized late-1960s kind of British pop song whose saving grace is the Pete Townshend–esque chords in the choruses. The PSG keeps the musical structure but modernizes it, and if you didn't read the credits, you could very well think it was an original because the subject matter is well within Patti's beliefs on the power, importance, and influence of rock and roll and serves as her reflection and witness on the loss of the greats in her personal pantheon.

"Privilege" is a declaration and a warning of the potential dangers of fame in an "Icarus flying too close to the sun" kind of way. There's a coda where Patti chants, "I'm so young, so goddamn young," before downshifting and reciting Psalm 23 at the end, concluding with a triumphant assertion "Goddamn, goddamn, here I am."

"We Three" is a Bowery torch song, down to the key change and the almost-barrelhouse piano. One of Patti's secret weapons is her ability to step into the shoes of the ingenue and convincingly deliver a ballad, whether one of her own, a classic from her childhood, or a contemporary hit like Debby Boone's "You Light Up My Life," which populated her setlists with surprising frequency after its 1977 release.[26] "We Three" packs a punch in the simplicity of its whispered first line: "Every Sunday I would go down to the bar where he played guitar."

The bar is CBGB and he is Tom Verlaine, so the song recounts a little piece of history as well. The album juxtaposes "We Three," which is the story of her overlapping relationships with Verlaine and Allen Lanier, with "25th Floor," which is the next chapter of "Because the Night," the story of Patti and Fred in their rooms at the then-fading Book Cadillac Hotel, once the tallest hotel in the world, in downtown Detroit. As I characterized it in a review of the record, " '25th Floor' is about what happens when the woman in 'Because The Night' takes out a match and lights the whole damn place on fire."[27] It's a song she wrote with Ivan Král that fairly bursts out of the grooves with its heavy classic rockness in the best possible way.

"High on Rebellion" is the counterpart to "Babelogue" in that it doesn't exist except as the coda fanning the flames of "25th Floor." And the album closes with the title track, ethereal and hymn-like, a mellow aftermath. If you fell asleep to side B, you would likely drop off before the last notes of "Easter." Church bells ring, Patti's voice is cracked, tender, yearning.

Before settling on *Easter* as the album's title, Patti had been advocating that the record be named after the song she and

Lenny believed should be the first single: "RnRN." In what seems like a naïveté born of a myopic stubbornness to see the wider world, Patti was absolutely certain that everyone would understand what she was trying to say because the lyrics of the song lay it out: Jesus Christ, Jackson Pollock, Jimi Hendrix, *outside of society*.

A handful of journalists tried to engage constructively with Patti (and, to a lesser degree, Lenny) on the treatise, but their answers mostly conveyed frustration that no one else was on their wavelength on this particular subject, that the problem wasn't the word but rather our unwillingness to understand how it was being used.

There are just so many other words.

The strongest criticisms came from journalists who had traditionally been on her side: Robert Christgau stated that her thoughts on this particular subject were "full of shit";[28] Nick Tosches, who styled himself as an outspoken "outlaw," said in his review of *Easter* that "the concept of artist as n——r is silly and trite";[29] and Dave Marsh wrote that "RnRN" "is an unpalatable chant because Smith doesn't understand the word's connotation, which is not outlawry but a particular kind of subjugation and humiliation that's antithetical to her motives."[30]

The song stayed in the setlist; in 1978, it often opened the show. Upon Patti's return to live performance, I am sure I am not the only person who wondered if she might have reconsidered the song, given the gift of time and reflection, but it was there from the very beginning. At my first show in 1979, that song was not part of the setlist, but it was back the first time I saw her after she returned to the music business in 1995, and I did not know what I was supposed to do. I was not going to sing that word—I was not going to even pretend that I did. (It is the feeling most Jewish kids have had to wrestle with singing Christmas carols at school that talk about Jesus; I moved my lips but didn't say the word.) As a white girl from Connecticut, I had the luxury of not thinking too hard about what it felt like to stand in a crowd of people yelling that word with their arms in the air, but I did not like it very much.

The poet and playwright Dael Orlandersmith, a long-time fan of Patti and punk rock, did not have the same privilege. In her essay, "Not a Rock N Roll N——r," she relates how it felt to stand in Central Park at a concert in 1976 and hear the song for the first time: "To hear it in that moment from someone who has defined you, who has spoken to you heart to heart, to hear it said from people that you're friendly, maybe even friends with, you're left speechless." She shares that in that moment she connected with another Black girl from the punk scene, who came over and said, "I can tell she doesn't mean it that way, but still, I don't like it. And look at all of them singing it, yelling it." Orlandersmith writes about how she considered throwing away her Patti Smith records, but ultimately did not. "I came to realize that she was racially naive, as opposed to being racist," she decides.[31] But she does not absolve Patti of responsibility.

It is true that "RnRN," performed live, will make your hair stand on end; it is always an electrifying moment if you aren't personally wounded by the use of the word. But God, in our current day and age, that seems duplicitous. I also understand that Patti feels strongly about the "outside of society" lyric and what it stands for. In 2016, she offered this explanation to the *Guardian*: "And what the crowd sings back to me is the line 'outside of society' because that's what it's about: gay kids, poets, people of colour, all of us. It was a big community of people outside of society. The song just means: 'Kicked out of there? Come here!' "[32] And yes! That is the line I resonated with then and continue to today. She turns rejection into affirmation: *we're here because we have nowhere else to go, but we also like it here.*

But she is also excluding every person for whom that word is violence.

No reasonable person thinks that Patti is racist or that the song is racist. But I don't understand how someone who is as committed to peace and justice as she is and who is smart and truly open to the expanse of the world would insist on continuing to perform a song featuring a word that is pejorative and hurtful to a large part of society. How, as an artist, do you not try something else?[33]

Easter reached number 20 on the *Billboard* 200. But even with that level of mainstream commercial success, there were still plenty of barriers manufactured by the music business establishment. The first was the cover. After two black-and-white covers, this time Patti worked with Lynn Goldsmith, who shot in color. The image chosen was an unposed shot from the end of the session, with Patti's arms over her head, adjusting her hair, wearing a plain cotton tank top with its tag sticking up, her gold necklace askew. It's a beautiful, serene image that projects strength, openness, and upward movement.

Once again, Patti sent her work into the world adorned with the imagery she felt best represented herself and her work, with zero consideration of how it would compare to anything on either side of it in the record store. It wasn't because Patti didn't care about her image — the outtakes from the Lynn Goldsmith shoot include an astonishing breadth of different treatments and concepts. But instead of being renowned for its beauty, quality, or creativity, the cover of *Easter* became controversial over the fact that Smith's uplifted arms displayed her unshaven underarm hair.

It is quite possibly the dumbest fucking thing that, in writing a book about one of our greatest artists, I have to spend a couple of paragraphs talking about the fact that one of the major issues surrounding one of her best and biggest-selling albums is that she did not choose to comply with patriarchal beauty standards and remove hair from a part of her body that American society has declared should be hairless for women. It wasn't even meant as any kind of feminist (or other) statement; Smith just didn't shave her armpit hair. (Again, one of the dumbest sentences in this entire book.) No male artist ever had to have a discussion with the head of their record label — with Clive Davis![34] — about the fact that having armpit hair on the cover meant that stores would probably refuse to stock the album or display it with the kind of prominence it deserved. (Apparently this was especially going to be a problem in the southern US markets.)

Yes, *every* female musician has had some conversation with someone at their record label about their appearance. But in my enormous database of articles about Patti Smith that I pulled together for this book, there are *ten* that come up when I type in "armpit hair." This is a woman who has been inducted into the Rock & Roll Hall of Fame and named a *Commandeur des Arts et des Lettres* in France. This is beyond absurd. It still manages to become a topic of conversation every time *Easter* is discussed, even as recently as 2018 in the pages of *Billboard* magazine.[35]

When the 1978 tour ended, Patti headed to Detroit, officially relocating to the Motor City to be with Fred "Sonic" Smith. Sonic was a member of the MC5, the Detroit proto-punk legends who invented — or at least perfected — guitar-based anarchy. The Five weren't just explosive, they were cataclysmic.

In March 1976, the Patti Smith Group was in Detroit to play a show at the Ford Auditorium. Lenny had invited Fred to the show and, before that, to a band reception held at one of Detroit's renowned diners, Lafayette Coney Island.[36] Lenny made the introductions, and Patti invited

Fred to play with them that night. Sonic joined them on-stage during the band's encore of the Who's "My Generation," and on an audience recording of that particular show — and maybe I'm reading into it because I know how the story ends — Patti sounds particularly inspired, and the audience reacts with the right amount of hometown enthusiasm when Fred comes onstage.

The two maintained their long-distance relationship (as alluded to in "Because the Night") until Fred asked her to come to Michigan and make a life with him. "Nothing seemed more vital to me than to join my love, whom I was destined to marry," Patti wrote in *M Train*, her second memoir, the book she would write after *Just Kids*.[37]

For the Patti Smith Group's fourth album, she called on her old friend, the musician and producer Todd Rundgren. Rundgren was working out of Bearsville Studios in Woodstock, New York, which meant that the PSG had to decamp upstate to work in winter 1978. The studio was the kind of hallowed and historical room that would appeal to Patti and Lenny especially. It was part of the larger Bearsville entertainment complex (including a restaurant and a theater and later, Rundgren's Utopia Video Studios) built by the '60s impresario Albert Grossman, who had managed both Bob Dylan and Janis Joplin. Patti and Todd had first met in Bearsville when she came up to visit Bob Neuwirth during the Band's *Stage Fright* sessions in 1970, and their friendship grew from there.

The two were now working together at a time when both of their stars were high in the rock and roll sky: Rundgren had produced Meat Loaf's *Bat Out of Hell* album in 1977, which was a huge commercial and artistic success (it went platinum in less than a year), and the PSG had had their first hit with "Because the Night." Patti trusted Rundgren personally and artistically, and she knew he had the technical side of production completely covered.

It's flat-out delightful that Patti chose to open *Wave* with "Frederick," a Motown-styled love song to her future husband, complete with multitrack harmonies. The direction she gave her producer for what would be the record's first single was that it be "so happy and accessible that everybody would want to dance." The classic girl group background vocals are, remarkably, all Patti, with Rundgren patiently directing her through the overdubs. "I have no ear for harmonies," Patti said later. "Todd's task was to help me widen my horizons, and he got me singing all these layered harmony parts." Similarly, Rundgren would push her to multitrack her vocals on the chorus of "Dancing Barefoot." Patti remembered, "In hindsight, it would have been a lot easier to get a nice girl singer in who could actually do it. Still, he got it out of me, and, in the end, I was quite proud of it."[38]

"Dancing Barefoot," the second single, is Ivan Král's greatest contribution to the band; it sounds and feels mysterious and atmospheric yet accessible. The images are clean and clear, and there's a shimmering depth in Patti's vocals that is part studio wizardry but mostly a credit to her growth as a vocalist. It has been her most-covered song, with a dozen or more recorded versions (U2's being the most well known). I remember hearing Patti's version played at New Wave dance nights during the 1980s and spinning around the club with my girlfriends; afterward, we would sit at a diner and talk about how we hoped she was happy out in Michigan and wondered if we would ever see her again.

I was the only one in my group of friends who had ever seen her live, not because I was older but because I was obsessed with rock and roll and started sneaking off to gigs at age fifteen. But there was a whole generation of women — the ones who would unironically spin around a bar's dance floor with their girlfriends — who adored Patti but were just a few years too young to have ever gotten to see her. We were sad about that but also united in our opinion that she owed us nothing and that she was entitled to whatever life she wanted to have. And then someone would inevitably make a comment about Fred "Sonic" Smith being hot, and that would break the spell.

The band's interpretation of 1960s folk-rock pioneers the Byrds' "So You Want to Be a Rock 'n' Roll Star" is inspired. The PSG style the song with a frenetic pace and urgency compared to the original's jangly peace-and-love vibe, and Patti delivers the vocals in a full-throated command worthy of Madison Square Garden. Jay Dee Daugherty kicks ass on this song, delivering a drumroll at the end that would make Keith Moon proud, and the guitars produce a glorious noise, which includes Patti, who delivers the final soaring feedback riff. Both versions of the song are meant to be sardonic, but Patti added a verse at the end with an extra twist that was both warning and exhortation. "This is the era where everybody creates," she declares, before shifting into lines about broken glass and "It's all a vicious game" instead of the original's "strange game."

The word choice was deliberate, in response to an attack on Patti's brother Todd, who was her tour manager, being hit in the face with a bottle by none other than the Sex Pistols' Sid Vicious. There's a note from Patti on the album's insert where she says that the first time she heard the song she didn't like it: "It seemed to say that in this field of honor, sooner or later, everybody gets hurt and I just didn't believe it."[39] At the time, it seemed like it was about Todd, whose injured face appeared alongside Patti's commentary, but in retrospect, it was the kind of clue (among many others) we should have noticed about her growing disillusionment with rock and roll as her chosen artistic form.

Lenny plays autoharp while Patti piously sings "Hymn" before closing side A with "Revenge," big, seductive, and slinking. With music from Ivan Král and Patti's lyrics and vocals perfectly embodying the song's title, "Revenge" presents the emotions of a woman who has been hurt and betrayed but whose scars have now healed and she is *moving on.*

Side B zigzags thematically, but the sonic consistency

brought by Rundgren's production (and later the mix) makes it gel. "Citizen Ship" is a straight-ahead, Ivan Král-style rock song, but it's also the story of Ivan's flight from his home country and how at that moment he was still stateless. (He would become a US citizen in 1981.) This is followed by the metaphysical vibe on "Seven Ways of Going," which is weighed down by an arrangement overloaded with New Age woo-woo (chimes! mystical echo on the keyboards!). Rundgren allegedly brought peyote to the studio to try to get the band into the right mood and I will blame that because stripped of adornment, the song is gorgeous live.

The oddly jagged "Broken Flag" carries the record into the last track, "Wave." When you listen on headphones it feels like Patti is in the room with you, talking to you, and Richard managed to get a Moog synthesizer to sound like ocean waves. Patti had a clear vision of how she wanted the song to sound, so Rundgren turned the board over to her (with an engineer to assist), and she ended up mixing the track herself. The song was written as a tribute to Pope John Paul I, whose image adorned the fan club fliers handed out at concerts during the summer. "He was just such a pastoral, beautiful man and he died so quickly," Patti said. "I really believed that he would have been a revolutionary Pope, had he lived."[40]

The band toured the record in spring '79, leaning for the first time toward larger venues. The PSG's final show in the

United States took place on August 11 at the Wollman Rink in Central Park, the band's third appearance there. It rained and rained; everyone got soaked waiting on line, and ultimately, the sold-out show would be cut short because the stage did not offer much protection from the elements. As the name indicates, Wollman was an ice-skating rink in the winter; this meant that when it rained in the summer during the concert series, the floor drained poorly and would be full of random large and small puddles, which is why everyone stood on their chairs or in the aisles during the show.

Patti opened by dedicating the first number to the people who slept overnight in the park to make sure they were first in line to get in, noting that she had done the same thing ten years earlier in order to see Little Richard.[41] She didn't get in because the show had sold out, so she just went and sat on the rocks.

If you say "the rocks" to anyone who ever went to a concert at Wollman, they know exactly what you are talking about: the rink was surrounded by these massive outcroppings of sparkling, mica-encrusted Manhattan schist that are all over Central Park. There was nothing like seeing a concert there because you were surrounded by trees, the gigantic rocks, and the city skyline, which, of course, lit up once the sun went down. It is one of those images tattooed on the inside of my eyelids; I would sit there slightly amazed that I was in the middle of the greatest city in the world and that this was happening. It's important to mention that the concert series held at the rink, which operated under different names throughout its history, was general admission and insanely reasonable: in 1979, tickets were priced at $4.50 for the orchestra and $2.50 upstairs. And if you didn't have that? The rocks.

Although I did not sleep overnight in Central Park, this was my first Patti Smith Group show in what I thought would be the glorious beginning of my PSG concert-going career. (I made up for it later.)

Later that night, the band played a "secret" show at CB's (though it seemed like every person inside Wollman knew about it). I did not go, but there is a tape: Patti's voice is tattered and ragged; she sounds exhausted but happy to be there, still. This show was recorded for the *King Biscuit Flower Hour*, a live concert syndication network for FM radio, and the setlist is a fair representation of an average 1979 show, from Patti's chats with the audience ("So what's going on tonight? Anybody at the Park today? Don't forget what I said about drinking some hot tea tomorrow.") to the balance of *Wave* material versus older albums and covers. (Conspicuously absent is "Because the Night," and I want to believe it's because there's *that guy* in the audience yelling "*Bruuuccceeee*" all night.)

Looking at the known setlists from the tour, I'm most struck by how Patti doggedly maintained a large number of songs from *Wave*, sometimes as many as eight. It might seem obvious that a band would want to be showcasing their new material on a tour to promote their latest album, but they wouldn't have been the first artist to get on the road and then ditch some of the challenging, newer material in favor of older material more familiar to fans.

But she stayed with these expansive versions of "Seven Ways of Going" or the performances of "Broken Flag," which I think mostly begged for a better place in the set — and they certainly tried to find where that space was, once sandwiching it between "Because the Night" and "Frederick" and other times positioning it on either side of that utterly delightful one-two punch (which I was so incredibly glad that Patti just let happen: *yes, I am going to play my big hits that you can dance to back-to-back. Deal with it*).

That segue is one of the moments I remember from the Central Park show, back in the days where setlists didn't appear on the internet as the concert was underway, that moment of pure joy when they went from "Because the Night" into "Frederick" and the linking synapses of "hits!" and "thematically connected!" and I danced happily atop my rusty, dented folding chair.

But not all the 1979 shows were as strong as Wollman, and some were downright terrible, an assertion backed up by reviews from writers familiar with her work and fact-checked against audience recordings. A review of the concert in St. Paul describes her as "in a dispirited, tired state" before ending with "What we learned on Wednesday night was that on a bad night, Patti Smith *is* pretty bad."[42] A review of a San Francisco poetry reading called it "an extended exercise in acute boredom."[43] These glaring inconsistencies are easy to understand: she was done and she was ready for it to be over. But I also can see the edges of a mindset she later explained by saying, "I was just completely arrogant. I'm not trying to be overly apologetic for my behavior — I wasn't evil. The lifestyle I had was one that lent itself to becoming more and more self-involved."[44]

The band headed for Europe at the end of August for a run of eight dates in France, England, the Netherlands, and Germany. The venues were all larger than usual, arenas and small stadiums with capacities ranging anywhere from twelve thousand to eighty thousand. The British date was at Wembley Arena, where they appeared with no support act and instead played two long sets. The reviews from that gig are soul crushingly negative from a music press that was horrified by *Wave* and felt that Patti and the band had let down the side, had betrayed the audience's faith, and had totally veered off course.

In some ways, they weren't wrong. The distance between US punk and UK punk had always been large, with the UK bands having more in common with each other, and the US bands sharing just about nothing except intent and origin. But UK punk was heading in another direction, and Patti and the band were, in the British critics' minds, still very much stuck in the same kind of past that punk was a reaction to and no longer moving forward.

Florence, Italy (AP): A concert Monday night by U.S. punk rock star Patti Smith went well until the American flag was hoisted during an encore. Riots and bottle throwing ripped through the crowd of 80,000, one of the country's largest rock audiences ever.

Officials said the rioting was instigated by leftist extremists who viewed the flag-raising as a provocation.[45]

When the Patti Smith Group arrived in Italy to perform two concerts in Bologna and Florence, they were the first international group to have played in the country since 1977 due to political instability. The fact that they only performed two shows meant that Italian fans traveled from all over the country. The venues were uninspiring, generic European football stadiums, and the audiences were exponentially larger than anything the band had ever faced: seventy thousand in Bologna and eighty thousand in Florence. It's tough to ask the audience how they're doing or keep their attention during a free jazz–inspired clarinet solo when they're behind chain-link fence several yards from the stage.

But the scope and the unprecedented nature of the concerts are the reasons Patti and the band were thrust into an environment upon arrival that they could not possibly have expected: paparazzi pursuing them, hundreds of girls dressed like Patti on the cover of *Horses* following them in the streets, television reporters sitting in the lobby waiting, bomb threats being called into the concerts, opportunists asking for the band to support or endorse politicians or political parties, and heavy security just waiting for a chance to work out their frustration on some excited Italian teenagers.

Even though her manager urged Patti to not display the American flag — it belonged to her brother Todd from his time in the Marines — behind the band as they usually did, she did it anyway. This was not the reason that the audience in Florence invaded the stage or that the carabinieri didn't like the band and were unnecessarily aggressive toward them, but it certainly did not help. Patti canceled the press conference scheduled to be held after the show, the band flew back to the United States, and Patti returned home to Detroit.

If Patti had not gone on hiatus shortly after returning to the States, the band's final shows in Italy would have been a dramatic footnote, a good story to tell. Instead, for years, the riot in Florence was presented as the reason everything ended for the Patti Smith Group. Eighty thousand rock and roll fans taking over the stage is a tangible, easy explanation for the media and fans, and it is easier to believe than the notion that a grown woman might decide to marry her soulmate and try to lead a normal life.

The clues were all over *Wave* and, in hindsight, there were plenty before that as well, but as Lisa Robinson noted in a 1996 interview with Patti, "Americans really don't understand turning away from fame."[46] There's also a piece of this that comes from women not being trusted as reliable narrators of our own lives. No matter how many times Patti explained why she was stepping away, no one believed her: there had to be another reason.

She told Robinson, "Being famous wasn't my prime directive; my prime directive had always been the work." She explained that much like the avalanche of offers after her St. Mark's Church reading in 1971, by the late 1970s she had been deluged with opportunities: "I was so successful that things were starting to come very easy to me. Things that people have to struggle really hard for: Art galleries and art museums in Europe wanted to show my work, all kinds of publishers called, people wanted me to do movies, and I really thought a lot of it wasn't necessarily based on merit. Once you get to a certain level of fame, you just get a lot of stuff handed to you." It was the reminder behind the lightning bolt tattoo she got from Vali: "I just didn't feel it was right, and I also felt the quality of my work—both performance and writing—was not as high as it could be."[47]

But in 1980, the message being sent through small mentions in the "Random Notes" sections of music magazines was that Patti Smith had left the music business and moved to Detroit—Detroit! of all places, a city abandoned and decaying—to set up house with Fred "Sonic" Smith. What about being a rebel, what about being an iconoclast, what happened to the field marshal? There was no empathy, no attempt to look at the situation through a humane or logical lens. She was thirty-four years old, had released four albums, published a handful of poetry books, exhibited in multiple art exhibits, had a top-ten single, opened for the

Rolling Stones and the Grateful Dead, toured America and Europe. That is not an exhaustive list, and yet, by any metric, that is a significant body of work, and it would continue to influence people for decades. None of that seemed to matter any longer.

I was annoyed because I was finally old enough to go to concerts without resorting to elaborate subterfuge. But it was also foreboding on another level, watching the mostly male music press turn on a woman who said "no" with finality and proceeded to diminish and dismiss her work of having children and raising a family. It hasn't stopped.

— 3 —

JUST BUMMING AROUND

Q: How do you feel about boys from the Midwest?
A: I like boys from Detroit.[1]

In March 1980, Patti Smith and Fred Smith were married at the Mariner's Church in downtown Detroit, just steps from the Detroit River.[2] In a photograph that Patti has publicly shared, the two are standing in the park in front of the church; they look like typical newlyweds, nervous but happy. Lisa Robinson would report that the only attendees were the parents of the bride and groom—and because it was a Lisa Robinson column, she helpfully added that "and the bride wore an antique white wedding gown and ballet slippers."[3]

In June, Lenny Kaye and Richard Sohl came to Detroit to appear with Patti, Fred, and members of Sonic's Rendezvous Band in a benefit for the Detroit Symphony Orchestra, the second such benefit Patti and Fred had taken part in. It was an ambitious and far-out evening of rock and roll, multimedia, and poetry, which concluded with a thirteen-minute version of Sonic's Detroit anthem "City

Slang." But if folks thought this reunion was some kind of harbinger for the future, they would have been incorrect.

Andy Schwartz at the *New York Rocker* spoke to Lenny Kaye in April 1981 for an article in the magazine's "fifth-anniversary" issue, the anniversary in question being the advent of CBGB's downtown scene. In the interview, Lenny confirmed that while he was still in touch with Patti, he had "given up on the idea of the PSG ever reforming 'like it was in the '70s.' " Schwartz further described Patti's situation as "the self-imposed exile of Patti Smith to Detroit, where she married guitarist Fred 'Sonic' Smith and settled into her own version of domesticity."[4]

The pattern is familiar: the same people angry that Patti didn't exist within the world in a shape of their choosing were now angry that she chose to not speak to them. They resented her presence, but when she chose to remove herself from the public discourse — she silenced *herself* — they were angry and resentful because she did so of her own accord and desire. Once again, she was not conforming to their dictates.

As a fan, I was sad that now that I was old enough to see as many Patti Smith shows as my heart desired, I didn't have the chance. But I was also livid that so many journalists and other musicians, people who knew her, were ready to dismiss the work she had already done and to vacate her worth to them as a human being because she fell in love and did what she wanted to do. Patti never considered herself a feminist, but I considered myself one, and to me, the whole point of feminism was to make sure that a woman could make her own choices. Wasn't she doing that?

We get a glimpse of Patti's early time in Michigan in *M Train*. Living in the then-ancient Book Cadillac Hotel in downtown Detroit (the building referenced in "25th Floor" on *Easter*), hanging out at the Arcade Bar across the street, steps from Lafayette Coney Island where the two of them first met. Those passages in *M Train* convey the feeling of intimate insularity inside a honeymoon, Fred and Patti building their own world, one without limits or expiration dates. There was no demand from the record company to make a new record, no expectation of having to go on the road and tour to promote it. She had told Clive Davis that she was taking a break, and, remarkably, he honored that.

Rock and roll as an industry, to this day, does not willingly make room for its creators to live a life, a scenario all the more ironic as it's the artist's life that fuels their art, which is the very thing that makes them a valued commodity. There is a machine of promoters and distributors and publicists, an ecosphere of venues and road crews and per diems, of lifestyles built around expectations of a continuous supply of More. There are bonuses. There are shareholders. But mostly, it is simply capitalism at work, and capitalism relies on this momentum to keep things going. No one in their right mind would walk away from fame, success, power, and money, right?

Patti and Fred were going to try.

*   *   *

St. Clair Shores, Michigan, is a suburb thirteen miles north-east of downtown Detroit. As the city's name indicates, it's on the edge of Lake St. Clair, one of the bodies of water that connects Lake Erie with Lake Huron. The town has a decided nautical focus, with marine supply stores and various waterfront seafood eateries. The streets between Jefferson Avenue (the main thoroughfare that runs all the way down to Detroit) and the lake are ringed with ca-nals. It is neat and quiet; houses are adorned with wooden seagulls and lighthouses and anchors. The area, once mostly working-class, has become more economically di-verse over the decades; larger houses or yards with enor-mous boats parked out front are not unusual nowadays.

Beach Street is found toward the southern end of town. The houses are mostly modestly sized ranch or two-story bungalows. They all have canal access in their backyards; you can have a boat docked right outside your back-door, and many residents do. (Local legend likes to insist that these portals were used by bootleggers back when they rolled barrels of hooch across the frozen lake from Canada.)[5]

By a long shot, 22501 Beach Street is the coolest house on the street. While it has a modest yard and a dock out back and isn't out of proportion with the rest of the neighbor-hood, the house is essentially a tiny English castle. There's a turret, leaded windows, and an arched stone doorway holding a wooden door that bears Gothic-looking iron hardware. This is the house Patti and Fred Smith settled into for their new life in a Detroit suburb marked by parks and neighbors and good schools, the kind of place where you could pursue a "normal" life and raise a family.

It was curious to discover the mundanity of St. Clair Shores. It was not what I was expecting after all those years reading about Patti's life in Detroit. I went looking for the house precisely because the stories and photographs made it seem like she was living in the middle of nowhere, not on a suburban residential street about a five-minute walk from a 7-Eleven, the Harbor Lanes Bowling Center, and Detroit's Finest Coney Island.

Admittedly, the Smiths were not the strongest advocates of yard maintenance, and so the trees and shrubbery grew wild. But still, it's not a remote, desolate farmhouse, which was the impression from the small glimpses we got over the years. Photos of Patti taken outside the house during her time in Michigan were only adding to the myth that she and Fred were some kind of hermits; I get why a photographer would want the very photogenic house in the background, but the pictures that would end up being used, consciously or unconsciously, were always these dramatic black-and-white images of Patti framed by an ivy-covered wall and a large unruly hedge that didn't convey the reality of the situation and instead made you feel like she was a princess locked away at the top of the castle.

In 1994, Lisa Robinson asked Patti if she thought that she would live in Detroit for as long as she did. She replied, "When I went there, I didn't think we were going to live as isolated as we did."[6] She had neighbors immediately adjacent, but I understand what she means; in New York City, you can walk anywhere, you have bookstores and coffee shops and movie theaters and the hum of the city all around you twenty-four hours a day. You can get on a bus or a subway or hail a taxi and easily be somewhere else. The suburbs aren't a great place to live if you can't drive — Patti didn't have a license and has never driven — and it's even more isolating if you're one of those people who sticks out like a sore thumb just by existing.

It might not make sense from the outside, stepping away from what might seem to others to be a glorious way of life. But those years of quiet and peace that Patti describes in *M Train* — driving around the country with Fred, stopping wherever they wanted, and pursuing their own interests, even (and especially) if those interests were personal and not particularly profitable — feel romantic, brave, exciting, and maybe even a little terrifying. Fred decided he wanted to learn to fly. Beginning at the Wright Brothers National Memorial in Kill Devil Hills, North Carolina, they drove down the coastline to Florida, stopping at flight schools. They eventually holed up in St. Augustine, and Fred flew while she wrote. They thought about buying a boat or even a decommissioned lighthouse. It was part of an ethos Patti termed "the clock with no hands," named for an old railway clock that hung on the wall in the Arcade Bar. "We reserved the right to ignore the hands that kept on turning," she wrote in *M Train*, ordering their life to a rhythm and pace that suited them. Most of us are not that brave.[7]

None of this journey feels out of character for Patti; in it you can see the Beat poets looking for America, Bob Dylan retreating from the public eye after his motorcycle accident, Robert Frank exploring the country through his unfiltered lens, Rimbaud wandering through Europe, the East Indies, and ultimately, Abyssinia. Those early married years feel like a return to the way she had interacted with her life and her art before she had become immersed in rock and roll; she studied different subjects and wrote and thought and dreamed. Once again, it was just about the work.

In a notebook of Patti's now in the archives of the New York Public Library, there's a poem called "Just bumming around" that reads as though it's a response to much of the questioning about what, exactly, she and Fred were doing with their free time:

> I met my baby in front of a radiator
> I asked him
> what you doing
> me—I'm bumming around
> let me bum around with you[8]

In 2015, she shared this frustration with journalist Alan Light:

> People kept saying "Well, you didn't do anything in the 80s," and I just want to get Elvis Presley's gun out and shoot the television out of their soul. How could you say that? The conceit of people, to think that if they're not reading about you in a newspaper or magazine, then you're not doing anything. I'm not a celebrity, I'm a worker. I've always worked. I was working before people read anything about me, and the day they stopped reading about me, I was doing even more work.[9]

It certainly appeared punitive and to some extent, retaliatory, especially given much of the reaction to the first piece of work that would arrive during this period of time, *Dream of Life*.

In June 1988, a new record arrived in the Patti Smith section of the record store. Featuring ten songs, all cowritten by Smith (Patricia) and Smith (Sonic), *Dream of Life* was a record that many people had been hoping and waiting for. Along for the ride were Jay Dee Daugherty and Richard Sohl from the PSG. Gary Rasmussen (from Sonic's Rendezvous) and Kasim Sulton (known for his work in Todd Rundgren's Utopia, as well as a vast amount of session work) shared bass duties and Fred and Jimmy Iovine shared the production credit. The Smiths worked on the record in pieces over the years, working around Patti's unexpected pregnancy with her second child, Jesse Paris Smith, in 1986.[10]

The cover of the record was one of the last times Patti would work with Robert Mapplethorpe, who died of complications from AIDS in spring 1989. As always, he saw and used natural light in an effective and powerful way, photographing her outside in a warm afternoon sunlight that both flattered Patti and created a textured, visually engaging background against the leaves of the palm tree behind her. It looks like Patti Smith and does not try to obfuscate the fact that she was now in her forties. In an industry obsessed with youth, the cover photo for *Dream of Life* constituted a quietly radical act.

The challenge *Dream of Life* would face was that with its release, Patti Smith was, once again, violating an extensive list of unspoken norms just by being a working artist. She wasn't nineteen years old, high on Dylan and Baudelaire, the Rolling Stones and Rimbaud. Patti was forty-two years old, married, and the mother of two young children. If she had been writing songs in the same vein as her earlier body of work it would have been disinguous, a betrayal of her artistic ethos. It's also highly unlikely she would have been emotionally capable of sitting down and trying to deliberately inhabit that space again. In several of her early "return" readings, she got tongue-tied over certain lines of poetry and more than once made a comment like, "I have no idea what that's about" or "I was a wordy little something, wasn't I?" She so deliberately took leave of that era of her life and work that going back to it would have been odd in the extreme.

Thematically, one can draw very direct lines between the work on this record and all the albums that would follow. She's writing about relationships and friendship, birth and loss, the condition of the planet, peace and justice, love and fate. The challenge was that it was not what many people were expecting from Patti Smith. But did anyone insist on comparing *Magic and Loss*, Lou Reed's 1992 dissection of mortality, illness, and death, to *Transformer*, his 1972 glam/art-rock outing produced by David Bowie? They're both great albums, but could not be more different in subject, style, mood, instrumentation, production, thematic arc, or any other element.

Dream of Life was also about the collaboration between Patti Smith and Fred Smith, and Patti emphasized the importance of the duality of the work in the few interviews she gave. "Working with Fred is very important to me. Our album represents us working together," she told Mary Ann Cassata in 1988. "We have a lot of other ideas and songs we haven't done yet. Many songs. We're looking into the future with some other works. We have achieved what we wanted with this album. What we wanted to do was a piece of work together that addressed the things we cared about."[11] And as Patti wrote in *Complete*, "This was an extremely difficult album to create, with two highly self-critical people trying to please themselves as well as each other."[12] It was intended to be the beginning of their public expression as musicians working together, but critics were more interested in the couple's plans for touring or performance or other future records than in the album in front of them.

Dream of Life would have been worth it for its title track alone: the opening bars of "People Have the Power" will always bring you to attention, will always make you sit up and take notice. That soul-satisfying, martial, deliberate call-to-arms drum roll is courtesy of Jay Dee Daugherty, who was always a great drummer for Patti, but now, after working with other bands and doing sessions for a decade, he is a great drummer, period. "People Have the Power" did not get the praise it rightly deserved when it came out, but there were those who heard its message and would remember it.

"Going Under" fools you until the bridge, when it expands and pulls you in. "Up There Down There" is a great showcase for both Fred and Patti and how they work together — Fred begins the song with a distinctive riff that threads its way back through the song and accompanies Patti's vocal with a melodic guitar counterpoint that runs underneath. Her vocal delivery is particularly inspired: you hear the old Patti drawl, but the tone of her address is firm, and she works in a playful, mild Dylan imitation in the middle eight. It's hilarious and adorable.

Although *Dream of Life* came out at a time in which albums were still sequenced with a side A and side B in mind, it benefited from the move to compact disc; the segue from "Paths That Cross" (the end of side A) to "Dream of Life" (the beginning of side B) works beautifully. "Paths That Cross," written for Robert Mapplethorpe's partner (and Patti's friend) Sam Wagstaff, who passed in 1987, is achingly sad, while the title track is a progression in the phases of mourning, quietly anchored by a guitar line that skirts along the edges of grief.

And "Going Under" could be part of an unintentional trilogy, the metaphor of water as infinity and eternity. There's even a spoken-word bridge that feels a bit like the Shangri-Las more than anything. "Going Under" is one of Patti's best vocal performances on a record chock-full of them. Whatever complaints there might be with overproduction and guitars and synthesizers, Patti's voice, which has only improved with rest and better use, is balanced perfectly in every single song.

I hear the continuation of "Frederick" in "Looking for You," both in sound and feeling. And the record closes shop beautifully with "The Jackson Song," a lullaby written for their first child. This is another track that has aged beautifully live, which speaks to the strength of the composition, as "lullaby" and "rock concert" are completely diametrical. "Oh, my parents put a *lot* of love into that song," said Jackson Smith in 2004. "When I was in high school and trying to be cool and just a regular teenage boy, my friends would be like [in mock-sarcastic voice] 'Oh, I heard "The Jackson Song!" ' "[13]

*   *   *

The album's most enduring legacy has a very prosaic origin. Patti loves to tell the story about how Fred walked into the kitchen in St. Clair Shores, declaring "People have the power!" and exhorting Patti to write a song with that title. Sometimes she is "peelin' potatoes," other times just "doing KP," but the setting is always described, I think, because of its commonality: that one can do great work even while living a quiet life at home, that amazing things can arise out of the mundane.

Although it is unquestionably a great rock and roll anthem, the best way to experience "People Have the Power" might be by listening to Patti read it with no instrumental accompaniment. It's there you have the chance to hear the art and skill in the lyrics, her skill at compression and distillation to key moments. As she always does, even without music she imparts movement and emotion in the words, and there's an even greater sense of urgency conveyed:

> Listen. I believe everything we dream
> Can come to pass through our union
> We can turn the earth around
> We can turn the earth's revolution

To write the song, Patti listened to the speeches of Rev. Jesse Jackson, conferred with her sister Linda about relevant Bible verses, and pulled in threads of current events, specifically the Soviet-Afghan War. The task that Fred had set out wasn't trivial: writing lyrics for something destined to be anthemic puts a tremendous weight on the writer. This isn't a poem that was turned into a song; "People Have the Power" was absolutely intended to be sung by as many voices as possible and to ring true with as many hearts as it could reach.

The song also stands as Patti's best vocal performance on the record. Her voice is strong and resonant, and you can feel her urging you on. The recorded version is performed and produced to sound large and expansive, but while the echo and the drum processor were common in 1988, those effects don't do the song any favors now. Fred's Rickenbacker jangles behind the vocals and I wish it had the chance to roar. I lament that Richard Sohl wasn't playing a grand piano or a Hammond B-3 organ, something more stirring than the synthesizer he's working on. But the strength of the song is that it still makes you want to drive down the road with your windows open or hold up a placard and march straight to City Hall.

It being 1988, Arista wanted a promotional video for MTV. The clip for "People Have the Power" is very, very Detroit, featuring downtown landmarks such as the Monument to Joe Louis, a twenty-four-foot-long bronze fist dedicated in 1986. The focal point was footage shot at the Detroit Institute of the Arts in front of the Detroit Industry Murals, painted by Diego Rivera in 1932 over a nine-month period. The crowning achievements of Rivera's career, they are the kind of deeply meaningful and influential art that someone would go out of their way to experience. Patti has told the story about how she took a bus to Detroit in 1973 to see the piece; on my own first visit to Detroit, visiting the Detroit Institute of Arts to see the murals was the second most important stop for me (the Motown Museum being the first).

The video also includes your standard 1980s shots of Patti standing in one place, dramatically lit, followed by shots of Sonic playing his Rickenbacker, equally dramatically lit. But the best and most Detroit of all the images in the video comes at the end, where you see Fred and Patti riding on a motorcycle downtown. They park, dismount, and enter the back of Lafayette Coney Island, the enduring Detroit landmark where they first met. Fred holds up two fingers to order as the song fades out.

I will be the first person to lament that the guitars are not bigger and louder on *Dream of Life*, but Fred "Sonic" Smith has a production credit, so we need to assume that the record sounded the way he wanted it to sound. I wish someone had disagreed with him because the guitar — his guitar! — is buried too far down in the mix. The second strike is the heavy use of the '80s favorite gadget, the synthesizer. Richard Sohl never stopped being poetic and fluid, but the synthesizer doesn't give him the kind of pause and control — a hallmark of his work — that he would get on a piano.

From a melodic and composition standpoint, while the

influences and reference points on the album might not have been au courant, all that shows is common sense. Robert Christgau wrote of the album, "The music is a little old-fashioned and quite simple, controlled but not machined, and the guitars sing."[14] You don't come back after being out of the game for a decade and try to emulate musicians with an entirely different vocabulary and reference point without sounding disingenuous.

Dream of Life emerged into the world alongside George Michael's *Faith*, *Hysteria* by Def Leppard, *Tougher Than Leather* by Run-DMC, and Guns N' Roses' *Appetite for Destruction*. What all those albums (and plenty of the other chart neighbors) had in common with *Dream of Life* was a production style, courtesy of our old friend Jimmy Iovine, whose star had continued to rise after *Easter*, now one of the industry's top record producers. On *Dream of Life*, there is compression and echo and an attempt to build a large sound that would be compatible with what else was on the radio; it's not any less cringeworthy from a production-values standpoint than anything else that was around.

In October 2004, the Vote for Change tour hit the road. Vote for Change was organized by the progressive advocacy group MoveOn and was designed to encourage people to register and vote. R.E.M. was part of the tour, on the same bill as Bruce Springsteen and the E Street Band. Michael Stipe, a diehard fan and one of many people who had reached out to Patti after Fred's death, kept bringing the audience greetings from Patti. For example, on October 2, he told an audience in Cleveland, "I'm really bad with dates, but she's really, really good with them, and she wanted me to remind everyone that today was Gandhi's birthday."[15]

A highlight of the show was Michael Stipe and Bruce Springsteen performing Patti's version of "Because the Night" during Springsteen's set. Michael sang Patti's lyrics with the ardor and enthusiasm of someone who had been listening to the song for years (which, of course, he had), and Springsteen and the E Street Band responded with their usual verve and energy.

But it was "People Have the Power" as the closing number, featuring all the musicians, that would create the kind of galvanizing, unifying moment the concerts were meant to generate. Michael took the first and final verses, which kept the energy high (especially since he accompanied it with some trademark Stipe-ian dance moves) and provided enough structure to ensure the song wouldn't degenerate into a Rock & Roll Hall of Fame Induction Ceremony jam session kind of mess.

According to Springsteen, the idea to close the shows with "People Have the Power" came, perhaps unsurprisingly, from Stipe. "The song was just tremendous at the end of the show every night. It's one of Patti's greatest songs, if, in some ways, maybe her greatest. . . . It takes a big song to end a big night, where there are supposedly big stakes on the table. And that song could carry the weight."[16]

Although "People Have the Power" had certainly been

sung at protests or other political events in the past, its prominence in the Vote for Change tour exposed a younger demographic to this song. It is irksome that it took sixteen years for it to enter the cultural zeitgeist in a way it should have upon its release. It's frustrating that it happened because a couple of famous men believed in the song (and the artist) and had the prominence to effect this kind of exposure, but equally true is that the song's inherent power is what allowed it to rise. The result is what the song's authors had hoped for. "Fred and I didn't write 'People Have the Power' to be an obscure song," Patti told *Addicted to Noise* in 1997.[17]

Dream of Life, despite mostly positive reviews in major publications, did not gain the traction it should have. The record only got to number 65 on the *Billboard* 200 and "People Have the Power" didn't chart on the Hot 100 but did surface in the top twenty on a chart that focused on mainstream rock and roll radio stations. In terms of promotional tools to help the album along, Patti did a few interviews, there was the "People Have the Power" video, an electronic press kit was released that included an interview with Patti and some older footage, and that was it. But there was no tour, no television appearances, no radio station visits, none of the traditional promotion accompanying a record release.

Touring is hard work and takes a lot out of you physically, especially if you're not at Learjet-level fame. Patti told Lisa Robinson that she always had bronchitis when she was on the road back in the day, so it's not particularly surprising that she was hesitant to get in the van again.[18] More important, Patti and Fred did not want to take the kids on tour: "I know it's a trend to take your children with you on the road, and I know that maybe some people can handle it well, but I don't subscribe to that," she told a writer in 1995. "What really happens is your children end up being raised by nannies and friends and daycare people."[19]

Subsequently, there was a lot of grousing in the media about their refusal to go on the road, but did anyone ever lecture Tom Waits or Leonard Cohen, two artists who famously did not tour for years and years, that they shouldn't expect any success unless they agreed to play live shows or publicly instruct them on how they should manage their childcare while on the road? Did their lack of live performance become a major topic in interviews? Instead, it was lauded as an indicator of their artistic integrity or their inherent genius.

Patti Smith wasn't accepted by the mainstream in the 1970s, so it shouldn't have been all that surprising that the mainstream in the late 1980s wasn't interested in paying attention, but it certainly was just as disheartening. There was no attempt to examine her impact on contemporary bands or the culture as a whole.

In many ways, Patti's unceremonious return to the music business wasn't much different from that of any successful businesswoman who took time off in order to have children and then tried to come back to an equivalent professional level: instead of looking at her work and her impact and the quality of her contributions, all anyone saw was that she had gotten married, moved to the suburbs, and had two kids. The lack of success for the album felt like a personal slight to those of us who had never stopped being inspired by the work Patti had done.

It's also worth examining where Patti was in her life. She was married and a mother; she was no longer "available," even if her prior "availability" had only been in the vivid fantasies of tastemakers and other men — promoters, radio program directors, TV bookers — who had a direct impact on her success or failure. In 2014, Lisa Robinson observed, "Now that Yoko Ono, Patti Smith and Marina Abramovic are too old to be thought of as sexual in this culture, they get respect."[20] In 1988, Patti would not be granted even that, and the impact of the album's failure (by most conventional metrics) had a chilling effect on any future plans for more music. Patti was back, and then she was gone again.

After *Dream of Life*, the Smiths returned to Michigan and to their life as the parents of two young children. "I truly loved my family and our home, yet that spring I experienced a terrible and inexpressible melancholy," Patti would later write.[21] She had lost Sam Wagstaff and Robert Mapplethorpe, two beloved friends from her early striving days, and then Richard Sohl died from a heart attack in 1990.

Add the unenthusiastic reception for *Dream of Life* and you have an unsurprisingly fertile atmosphere for depression.

Patti had always turned to her work in times of crisis or unease, so it made sense that she would look to her poetry and longer-form prose—which she hadn't published yet but had been writing for years—as her creative focus. So, in 1992, when the iconoclastic imprint Hanuman Books came knocking, Patti agreed to write a small book for them, titled *Woolgathering*. Hanuman published pocket-sized, intensely colorful volumes, and she found herself charmed by their physical form. She would appear in a series alongside people like Warhol "superstar" (and fellow Max's backroom denizen) Candy Darling, William Burroughs, Grateful Dead lyricist Robert Hunter, and other similarly freethinking folk. It must have been gratifying to take her place once again in this particular lineage.

Woolgathering inhabits the same kind of space between dreams and reality that Smith would later explore in *Year of the Monkey*, the book that followed *M Train*. *Woolgathering* centers itself deeply within Patti's childhood home in New Jersey and veers between real life and imagination and how the two often converge in a child's mind. It was a small effort, but it buoyed both Patti and the small press, and she would agree to appear at a New York benefit reading in support of the book in the coming year. She would also accept a request from Andy Warhol's *Interview* magazine to write a poem to accompany a photo essay. These were small incursions back into public life, but meaningful ones to anyone who hoped *Dream of Life* indicated that she was ready to share her work with the world again.

Patti Smith, with ex-MC5 husband Fred Smith in tow, appears at the Nectarine on April 6. Even though they live in tranquil domestic bliss in the far eastern suburbs of Detroit, it is a big fucking deal that this non-victim of the 70's is playing Ann Arbor again.[22]

Out of nowhere in spring 1991 came an announcement of a live performance, featuring both Patti and Fred Smith, in a benefit on the last night of one of their favorite clubs in Ann Arbor. Back in the day, the Patti Smith Group played so reliably at the Second Chance (also known as Chances Are and then the Nectarine Ballroom) that locals joked about them being the house band, and Sonic's post-MC5 side project, Sonic's Rendezvous Band, was also a frequent flier. The club, a notable stop on the touring circuit in the '70s and '80s, enjoyed a reputation that extended beyond the Michigan borders. The venue was closing and becoming a dance club, and the owner, John Carver, called Fred Smith and asked if he and Patti would be willing to play closing night because their bands' performances had been some of his favorite memories.

Chez Smith agreed and called in some of their friends: Lenny Kaye and Jay Dee Daugherty came out from New York and were joined by locals Scott Morgan and Gary

Rasmussen from Sonic's Rendezvous and former Stooge Scott Asheton on drums. The evening was billed as "Happy Trails: A Concert to Benefit AIDS Featuring Fred 'Sonic' Smith and Patti Smith."

Yes. It was a big fucking deal. Fans drove hundreds of miles and endured lengthy bus journeys.[23] The club fielded media requests from all over the country. People who made it inside remember the club being packed and uncomfortable. Listening to the extant audience recordings, you can hear that; the crowd murmur is more like a roar, and people are *ready*. There are howls for Sonic, screams for Patti, other people yelling "All the way with Lenny Kaye," an old T-shirt slogan from the 1970s. Patti had warned the *Detroit Free Press* that people shouldn't expect too much: "It's important for people to know the night will be special, but not like a formal concert. It should be happily flawed."[24]

It's impossible to listen to the evening and not think about how this could have been the norm, had Patti and Fred gone on tour. Especially poignant is how Fred introduces his wife, possibly the only such moment they had: "Welcome to the Second Chance," Sonic greets the audience. "The first person I'd like to introduce, I met at a little coney island in Detroit called Lafayette Coney Island." The crowd applauds the restaurant with the appropriate Michigan level of enthusiasm. "If you're down that way, you might want to check it out," Sonic dryly acknowledges. "She was having a little pre-gig party, and I went just for the hot dogs and beer because I'd never really heard of her.

So we met, she invited me to their gig at the Ford Auditorium, we played a couple of songs, we played 'My Generation'; it was fun. One thing that struck me was how great she was with lyrics, and, of course, a little later on, I discovered her poetry. So, it's a pleasure to introduce to you tonight a good friend of mine: Patti Smith!"[25]

The audience response sounds like a crowd of twenty thousand. "All I can say is, if I win an Academy Award, it could never be this good," Patti responds. She gets through "Piss Factory" — which Susan Whitall, formerly the editor of *CREEM* but at the time writing for the *Detroit News*, described (not inaccurately) as "her poem about nonunion piecework"[26] — before a belligerent fellow yells for Fred several times. "Hey, buddy, why don't you go for a walk, get a cup of coffee, smoke a cigarette, come back in about fifteen minutes," she replies, shattering any illusion that somehow motherhood or the suburbs had diminished her in any way. She reads "Mitty" for Richard Sohl, calling out the recipe for "white java: Evian, Nescafé, too much milk." She finishes with an abridged version of "Babelfield," during which the crowd chatters impatiently, but they cheer enthusiastically at the end.

Sonic opens with his amazing composition "Sweet Nothing," later delivers a killer twelve-minute version of "Empty Heart," and offers a rendition of "Dangerous" that will light your speakers on fire right now. These are exceptionally good songs that were largely overlooked outside the immediate geographical area, and the band sounds more practiced and polished than you would expect after not having played live in many years.

Lenny Kaye absolutely kills a rendition of "For Your Love," evoking the memories of his PSG solo spots, before Patti rejoins the musicians onstage and we get to hear "My Generation." Now we've entered the world of what could have been: Lenny Kaye, Fred "Sonic" Smith, and Patti Smith onstage together. It's loud and messy and Patti forgets words and misses cues, but it is a glorious train wreck that we all should have been able to experience. Everyone — first and foremost, the people performing onstage.

Patti and Fred move into an acoustic interlude, singing "It's a Hard Rain's A-Gonna Fall," "Paths That Cross," and "Ghost Dance." While the crowd carries on noisily through the first two numbers, shortly into "Ghost Dance" they fall as silent as they've been all night. It's as good as any live version from back in the day — better, even, because the musicians have all grown in the ensuing years.

"People Have the Power" is the last number, and it's performed as more of a giant rock anthem than the protest spiritual it's since become — which is not a bad thing! Sonic deploys a harmonic effect on his guitar line on the chorus, similar to some of his work with Sonic's Rendezvous. It is huge and glorious. But it isn't really the last number after all; Patti and Fred return to sing the Roy Rogers/Dale Evans classic "Happy Trails," technically the name of the event.

Whitall was backstage after the show and reported this

delightful detail: "Fred 'Sonic' Smith whips his wallet open with lightning speed. Of course he has pictures of his 8-year-old. Baby pictures. 'He really wanted to come tonight,' Fred says wistfully. Earlier mother Patti had said: 'This just isn't the right place for children physically. Spiritually maybe. But there's too much smoke and noise.' "[27]

The concert raised $9,000 for Michigan AIDS networks. Patti took a moment during the show to explain who was benefiting from the evening, saying that everyone there should be sure to talk to their friends about HIV and AIDS and support anyone who might contract the disease. Rock and roll had not been a great supporter of this cause to that point, and in 1988, she told Lisa Robinson, "The most valuable thing about having any type of fame, or power, is how you use it to help your fellow man or help the planet or make people aware of certain things. . . . One thing that I was well aware of when I stopped in 1979 was that I wasn't using my position in a worthwhile way."[28]

The second glimmer of hope that Fred and Patti were ready to return was their song "It Takes Time," officially credited to both of them, appearing on the soundtrack of Wim Wenders's 1991 science fiction futurist drama *Until the End of the World*. Wenders asked many of his favorite musicians to record the kind of music they imagined they might be making at the end of the decade. There are few albums I played more in the early 1990s than the soundtrack to this film, which also included R.E.M., Laurie Anderson, Nick Cave and the Bad Seeds, U2, and others.

"It Takes Time" is a solemn, atmospheric dirge accompanied by spoken word from both Patti and Fred. The fresh, modern-sounding track, which feels more grounded in European rock and roll than American traditions, was warmly received, and it is not at all difficult to imagine that it sounds like Fred and Patti in their future artistic forms. "That's almost entirely his piece," Patti told Ben Edmonds in 1996. "Not only did he write the music and some of the poetry, he actually dictated how he wanted me to read my parts. Oh yeah, we had some friction, some healthy friction, in the recording of that song."[29]

The soundtrack album did well commercially due to the presence of R.E.M. (who had just released *Out of Time*, which turned them into an enormous international act) and U2 (who released their epic *Achtung Baby* around the same time), and Patti and Fred's track was almost always mentioned in reviews as a strong point. After the commercial disappointment of *Dream of Life*, the positive critical reception was a refreshing change. As a fan, I hoped "It Takes Time" was a harbinger of what they might be doing next.

The next trial balloon was a big one: in July 1993, Patti was announced as the first author in SummerStage literary events that summer. The SummerStage venue is essentially an enclosed outdoor space in Central Park with a stage at one side of it. You are out in the sun and the stars and have to deal with the weather, good or bad. For Patti, the space was packed solid on a steaming hot New York evening. Yet, in 1995, she would tell Evelyn McDonnell in the *Village Voice* that she worried no one would show up.[30]

The overwhelming joy of the crowd welcoming her back to her first reading in fourteen years transmits with crystal clarity through an audience recording from that day. As she takes the stage, there is loud, extended, enthusiastic applause, cries of "Welcome back!" and "Welcome home!" and general jubilation—even listening to it decades later, you can feel the emotion of the audience radiating outward.

"The streets are meltin', the sky is swelling, even the trees are rebelling," Patti greets the crowd, "but it is nothing, because I am here, I am still here! And I am armed. I have my dental floss and I have my spectacles. What a great-looking crowd! I know it's hot out there," she says. "We don't care!" shout multiple audience members. "We love you!"[31] There are yelled requests and more shouts of encouragement. "I can't do that piece yet. I'm too nervous," Patti responds to some more audience shouts. "I'm just gonna be honest, I'm just a little nervous. I'm going to read a little thing for ya so I can get my bearings straight. The Bering Strait!" The crowd laughs softly. "This is a little poem for Amelia Earhart," Patti says. There is definite applause in recognition, along with cries of "Siddown!"

But immediately after she finishes reading the poem from *Seventh Heaven*, she slips right into "Sixteen and time to pay off." The roar of recognition and elation in response to the opening line of "Piss Factory" is as heart-stopping as her utterance. She had clearly found her footing again, and the energy, humor, self-deprecating asides, and witty repartee with the crowd was all there. Patti read for an hour, fifteen pieces in total, old and new. "Mitty" is once again for Richard Sohl. "Song for Somalia" is half sung, half recited; it's followed by "Libya" and then "Babelfield." I wasn't there, but it sure sounded like she got a standing ovation after "Babelfield," a request she said came from her brother Todd.

The crowd is remarkably attentive and supportive, and Patti seems to lose her jitters once she's into the body of each poem, delivering her work with an authoritative command that shines with intensity but has a pause and a weight that you did not hear earlier in her career.

"A lot of things have happened since I've seen you last," she said. "A lot of wonderful things, and a lot of tough things, and, like many of you, I have lost friends, just like many of you have, from various things, and, of course, we know, especially in New York, a lot of us have lost friends to the AIDS virus.[32] I'd like to sing a little song that I wrote for my friend Robert Mapplethorpe shortly before he passed away. Let's think about our friends for a moment, and think about them good, because as it's been eloquently stated, the departed live on in the memory of the living."

Patti sings "Memorial Song" a cappella, and there is not

one utterance from the crowd. It is 1993, and it is New York City, and that sadly means that entirely too many in that audience have also lost friends, lovers, or relatives to AIDS. But there are two thousand people jammed into the SummerStage enclosure and no one is yelping for her attention or just to make themselves heard. They are with her the way they were back in the day when she would bring up Arthur Rimbaud's birthday or Jimi Hendrix's passing. But now we are older, and it is personal.

She recites "People Have the Power," increasing in intensity as she works her way through the text, the audience keeping quiet but then exploding in applause at the end. Patti then clearly needs to vamp to kill time for some reason that's not apparent and tells the audience that she needs to come up with some patter, which then releases the pent-up questions that everyone had kept stuffed inside their throats all night because they didn't want to ruin the moment:

You're all taking care of yourself, I trust, and each other—
HOW ARE THE KIDS?
The children are wonderful. They're happy, healthy children.
ARE YOU GOING TO TOUR?
Oh, yeah, I'm going on a ninety-city tour, Fred and I are going on a ninety-eight-city tour in two weeks.
WE'LL BE AT EVERY ONE. DO YOU GO TO THE SUPERMARKET?
Do I go to the supermarket? Let me *talk* supermarkets.

WHAT DO YOU LIKE TO LISTEN TO?
I like to listen to the laughter of my children.
DO YOU MISS NEW YORK?
I've always loved New York.
BUT DO YOU MISS IT?
I miss it sometimes. I miss New Jersey, even.

"Cowboy Truths," the piece for Sam Shepard from *Wool-gathering* (the evening was theoretically in support of the Hanuman Press book; there is a commemorative T-shirt from the evening to that effect), is the home stretch. She then sings a bit of "Think of Me" from *The Phantom of the Opera*. And then, unbelievably, she's talking about John Paul I — "He's walking along the beach, and I just happen to — be there" — and she does a spoken-word version of "Wave," which is both brave and amazing.

The "encore" is an a cappella "Paths That Cross," during which Patti loses her place, apparently because people in the audience are singing along too loudly. The crowd tries to help by feeding her lines; someone asks her if she can still spell "Gloria" after fourteen years; there's a shout for "You Light Up My Life." Patti gathers herself, starts again, sings the verse, then tells everyone to go home and drink some water.

I'm 100 percent sure they would have done anything she asked them to. I hope she went home understanding how deeply she was missed. We all hoped, yet again, that we would see her again soon.

*   *   *

March 1994 brought the release of *Early Work, 1970–1979*, an illustrated anthology of both published and unpublished work. It was a slim volume, carefully and, in my opinion, correctly curated. Just as *Babel* pulled together poems across her entire body of work at the time, *Early Work* does the same, with about half the pieces overlapping between the two volumes. This was the first published collection of Patti's work in decades, making her poetry easily accessible to a generation of music fans who had been told by their heroes that Patti Smith was the reason for their artistic (and sometimes actual) existence.

In the years since *Dream of Life*, U2 had released their cover of "Dancing Barefoot," and Michael Stipe of R.E.M. had told the story of the first time he listened to *Horses* and stayed up all night eating cherries and losing his mind. You could not turn on MTV without seeing 10,000 Maniacs' version of "Because the Night" from their *Unplugged* session. And any time a woman fronted a loud rock band, she would undoubtedly be compared to Patti in some fashion, whether it was Kathleen Hanna, PJ Harvey, Courtney Love, Mia Zapata, all the members of L7, Liz Phair—it did not matter. If there was a woman that wasn't hiding in the back playing keyboards, some lazy journalist would compare her to Patti Smith. (Hell, they still do.) The time seemed right for another record from Fred and Patti.

*   *   *

Sadly, this hope was never realized. Fred "Sonic" Smith left this earthly plane on November 4, 1994. The cause of death was heart failure; in 2002, Patti told the *New Yorker* that though he had been sick with liver and kidney problems, it seemed he was getting better, but then he relapsed. Patti writes about that week in *M Train*, how she went with her husband in an ambulance to the hospital the day before Halloween; how their daughter, Jesse, slept in her costume the next day, hoping that he would be home in time to see it. "I thought he would pull through, but he didn't make it," Patti said.[33]

His funeral was held at the Mariner's Church, where the two of them formally began their adventure fourteen years earlier, and he was interred in Detroit's Elmwood Cemetery, alongside Civil War soldiers, politicians, leaders of industry, abolitionists, and other notable Detroiters throughout history. His grave marker stands out amid the more conventional monuments, consisting of two small, rough-hewn stone monoliths, one engraved "Frederick D. Smith/Musician XX century," the other engraved with the word "Sonic." The stone came from Ireland, where it was a marker for nearby grounded ships. "My husband loved the sea, and I knew he would love that," Patti told the *Irish Times*. "His grave initially had no headstone, because I couldn't find something that I knew would be meaningful to him."[34] His resting place has become a pilgrimage site not just for those he left behind, but also for anyone who cared about his music. His gravesite is well visited, with visitors leaving guitar picks, 45-rpm adapters, coins, and other tokens of respect.

Over Thanksgiving that year, Patti went home to New Jersey and spent time with her family. Her brother, Todd, was encouraging Patti to move forward, make music, and go on tour. He had been her road manager in the 1970s, and he insisted that he would quit his job so he could resume that role. She told Neil Strauss, "I was just totally desolate, and he said, 'I'm going to get you back on your feet. You're going to go back to work. Working will help you.' He said, 'I'm going to be right there with you.' And that's the last time I saw him alive."[35] Shortly after the holiday, Todd Smith died of a stroke, exactly a month after Fred crossed over.

Patti was alone, with two young children, in a suburb, and she didn't know how to drive. But offers of help began to arrive, starting with friends of her brother, who drove out to Detroit to offer tangible support. Danny Goldberg, a music industry executive who had been hanging around Max's and writing about music in the '70s (and later managed Nirvana) called to ask if she needed a lawyer, which is how his wife, Rosemary Carroll, began managing Patti's affairs.[36] Michael Stipe of R.E.M. reached out in sympathy and appreciation, which ignited a friendship; later on, he coaxed her out into the world by inviting her to attend the band's shows. Goldberg offered Patti the use of his townhouse in New York for the December holidays since he and Carroll would be traveling; it would put her nearer to her parents and sisters, she wouldn't need a car to get around, and she would be surrounded by her old haunts and dear friends.

On New Year's Day 1995, the sanctuary at St. Mark's Church was packed. Every year, the Poetry Project held their annual New Year's Day Poetry Marathon, and this year would feature a particularly special homecoming. People really tried to be on their best behavior and act like it was just another marathon, but everyone had heard the rumors (or if they hadn't, they were clued in once they arrived), and the energy in the sanctuary was tangible. Patti stepped onto the dais once again with Lenny Kaye behind her and read "People Have the Power." And then, with Lenny on acoustic guitar, she sang "Ghost Dance."

"Somewhere around the second or third verse she lost her way in the song," he told the *New Yorker* in 2002, "and she turned to me and I gave her the chord at the top of the verse to ease her in. She took it, and at that moment I knew that we had made it to the other side."[37] People cried, held hands, put their arms around their friends, or just sat dumbfounded. We had missed her, we were sorry for her loss, and we were just so glad to see her and hear her again. So many people in that room had never heard her sing her songs.

The next call came from Allen Ginsberg. He asked her to join him in a benefit being held in Ann Arbor to support the Tibetan Buddhist group Jewel Heart, an organization dedicated to preserving Tibetan Buddhist culture. As she has shared several times since, he called her and said, "It is time to let go of your loved one and continue your life's celebration."[38] He also likely knew of her affinity with the Tibetan people's fight for independence (which she would explore further in a few years when she released *peace and noise* in 1997); she accepted.

Ginsberg began the evening, and after a short intermission — "after which we'll have an important rock & roll poet who took poetry from lofts, book shops and gallery performances, to the rock & roll world stage," he said[39] — it was Patti's turn. The introduction was as much for the student-heavy crowd (Ann Arbor being the home of the University of Michigan) as it was for Patti herself.

Her hair was in braids like on the cover of *Dream of Life*, and she wore an open-stitch black sweater, striped T-shirt, and jeans. (There's a black-and-white photo taken that day by Ginsberg available on the Allen Ginsberg Project website.)[40] She would later ask the crowd for their opinion on her outfit, self-effacingly describing it as "sort of mid-70's Tibetan grunge."[41] Her appearance lasted only half an hour, during which she read three poems — one inspired by the Dalai Lama, one for her sister Linda, and then "Florence," which she dedicated to her brother Todd and introduced by saying "I traveled with a rock and roll band in the '70s, and the last job we ever played was in Florence, Italy, in a big soccer arena."[42]

Finally, borrowing the musicians who backed Ginsberg, Patti announced she wanted to sing a song for her husband, whom, she said, "many of you knew and loved as Fred 'Sonic' Smith." She didn't choose one of her own songs but instead a version of Johnny Mathis's "The Twelfth of Never," a song about never-ending love. A journalist in attendance wrote, "While she sang, the entire Hill Auditorium held its breath."[43] It is the kind of ancient pop standard — not quite Great American Songbook, but at least *adjacent* — that Patti can always sing the hell out of.

Another song she can sing the hell out of is Nina Simone's "Don't Smoke in Bed," which Patti recorded in March 1995 for the *Ain't Nuthin' but a She Thing* benefit album. The record was one of the first of its kind to raise money for the Shirley Divers Foundation for Women, a breast cancer charity focused on clinical trials for women and girls, named for a former Sire Record executive who died of breast cancer in 1992. The contributors are all female artists, interpreting songs of their choosing. Melissa Etheridge, for example, covers Joan Armatrading, Annie Lennox takes on the Sugarcubes, and Patti interprets Nina Simone.

There's a prominent line in the album's credits: "We are all particularly honored to have worked with Patti Smith on this record." "It actually makes me feel like crying when people tell me I influenced them," she told *Addicted to Noise* at the end of June that year. "I think it's really nice of them to say that, because I know who my influences were, and how much they continue to mean to me, people like Bob Dylan, the Rolling Stones and Jim Morrison."[44]

The song was produced by Freddie Brooks, a local Detroit producer and music biz jack-of-all-trades, who had worked with Fred Smith on various projects and was someone Fred had trusted. Accompanying Patti on the track were members of local band Detroit Energy Asylum, whose lead singer, Carolyn Striho, was married to Brooks at the time. After Fred's death, Striho and Brooks made the effort to stay in contact with Patti and the children and offer support and encouragement. That encouragement evolved into helping her record the Nina Simone track for the benefit album, which then transitioned into Patti and the group rehearsing and playing music together.[45]

This led to a series of low-key outings at Detroit-area venues obviously designed to get Patti acclimated to being back onstage and build her confidence, leading up to her July "comeback" show in Toronto. In the early outings, Patti looks and sounds a little tentative, but she is warmly received by the audiences.

These sets deliberately included the hits — "Dancing Barefoot," "Because the Night" — but the first show at the Magic Bag just outside Detroit also included "Up There Down There," "About a Boy," and "Wild Leaves," none of which had been recorded yet. Detroit Energy Asylum was more jazz based, so the arrangements are slightly different from the recorded rock versions, but as a platform for Patti to find her performing feet again, the collaboration was perfect. "All of them are very heartful," Patti told Evelyn McDonnell in the *Village Voice*. "To give somebody access to your people is really generous. That group of people really cared about Fred, and they really wanted to help me get back to work. It's been good for getting me focused for this record."[46]

Also falling under the categories of (1) "heartful" and (2) "your people" was none other than Lenny Kaye. He came out to Michigan several times to help Patti work through the songs that she envisioned being part of the next album and piece together some of the initial concepts that Fred had gotten on tape. Lenny also played with her at a few of her first live outings, including a benefit at the Ark in Ann Arbor for Fred, providing moral support and helping her get ready to return to work. It was the field marshal and her lieutenant general gearing up again to head into battle.

— 4 —

SHE WALKED HOME

On July 5, 1995, Patti Smith walked onstage at the Phoenix Club in Toronto to play her first "official" headlining show since the end of the 1970s. She was backed by Lenny Kaye and Jay Dee Daugherty along with the members of Detroit Energy Asylum. The 1,350-capacity venue sold out instantly and a late show was added; it, too, sold out immediately. The performance would mark the start of the second half of her career.

So, it wasn't exactly shocking that Patti was greeted with a lengthy standing ovation. "Standing alone on a largely unadorned stage, Patti beamed with a huge grin, trying to get a word in to an audience that would not stop the deeply felt huzzahs," wrote a local music fan who attended the show. "That triumphant entrance was simply the first of many emotional moments from that night."[1] The show began with a handful of poems, then Lenny came out to do "Ghost Dance" with her. Detroit Energy Asylum then played a short set — clearly giving Patti space to breathe a bit — before Lenny and Jay Dee came out with Patti. They performed eight or so songs, along the lines of what Patti had been trying out back in Michigan, which included the hits but also tracks from *Dream of Life* and brand-new songs no one had heard yet.

Performing new material in front of people who have never seen you before *and* people who had been around back in the day was brave. She could have walked out on-stage and sung half a dozen PSG songs from the '70s and people would have been thrilled and written endless glowing reviews.

It wasn't that Patti was trying to re-create what she did in the '70s, it's that the essential characteristics of who she was as a performer hadn't changed. Her voice shakes with emotion as she sings "About a Boy," and you can feel her genuine grief over Kurt Cobain's death and the impact that would have on a generation of music fans. She sounds delighted to be singing "Because the Night" again, and she's rightfully trying to make "People Have the Power" into the hit it would become. Her setlist instincts are still on point; she knows how she wants to build a show emotionally, and she still had access to that particular brand of magic.

If you had seen her in the 1970s, you would nod your head and think, "Yes, this is exactly what it was like." If you had never seen her but spent hours thinking about what it would be like, you would walk out with your head spinning because it would be exactly what you thought it would be.

At the end of the month, Patti performed again at Summer-Stage in New York, this time in front of a crowd of around nine thousand people, according to the *New York Times*. "Oh, I never left," she tells the crowd, in response to the shouts of "Welcome back!" "I shall not return because I was never gone. I was in disguise, and I was checking you out all these years. And you know what I think? You done good!"[2]

It was another family effort, including her sister Kimberly playing acoustic guitar; her good friend Janet Hamill, the oratory poet; plus Lenny and new addition Tony Shanahan, who would soon be part of the extended clan. Patti is nervous but more assured than she had been in 1993, easily sparring with the audience. She comes out with a copy of *Early Work*, and some hambones in the audience felt the need to yell for "Gloria." Patti retorts, "Personally, if you want to hear those songs, learn them yourself!"

She mediates a situation where someone in the crowd is standing and blocking the view of the stage and then dedicates "Land" to Robert Mapplethorpe. It shouldn't be a huge surprise that "Land" in its spoken-word form is equally as enthralling as it is translated into rock and roll, but it is always a tremendous moment. She read about ten pieces, including "Dog Dream," "Ballad of a Bad Boy," and "Cowboy Truths."

Lenny and Tony join her for "Ghost Dance" and "Paths That Cross," and then she announces, "We'd like to do a song written by Fred 'Sonic' Smith for you all." The crowd knows what's up and cheers at the first few chords. It's more proclamatory than the declamatory posture that would come with time, but she sings "People Have the Power" with strength and intention, and the audience — which has never had the chance to do this before! — picks up the chorus, getting louder as the song progresses. The collective energy rising through the repetition is still an incredible thing to hear twenty-five years later.

Once the applause dies down, Patti still has one thing on her mind: "I would also like to say that — many people, in various walks of life, speculate why I seem to be out of your eye for a while, and I can only say it is because I was privileged to be the wife of a great man, and I'd like to sing a little song for him." With that, she closes the night with "Farewell Reel," a song yet to be released, accompanying herself on guitar. She stumbles toward the end, stops, takes a breath. The crowd murmurs, "It's okay," and Patti responds, "Oh, I know that. You know why I know it's okay? That's because there's no other way."

She would later tell Holly George-Warren, "I've always found New York the most friendly town I've ever been in. That night, the response brought tears to my eyes."[3]

What prompted Patti's comments about speculation at SummerStage was the release of Patricia Morrisroe's authorized biography of Robert Mapplethorpe, published at the beginning of June. Given the degree to which Patti was involved in his life, she was both source and subject. Morrisroe received a great deal of criticism for the sensational nature of her writing and her focus on Mapplethorpe's lifestyle over his art. She also represented Patti and Fred's relationship as one in which they were not equals, and outright stated, "Mapplethorpe worried that Fred held too much influence over Patti, who seemingly needed to ask his permission for every move she made."[4] The book also made a big deal about Patti's dislike of phone calls and that people who came to Detroit to visit "couldn't find her."

"I was so in love with Fred, I was really unhappy when I wasn't with him, and he just said that he really thought we shouldn't be parted. So I made the decision we wouldn't be," she told Lisa Robinson in 1994. "It didn't take me months; I made the decision in one night and I never regretted it. I think what I did required more strength, more independence and more depth of character than not doing it."[5]

To have to deal with this backlash, which turned her and Robert's relationship into tabloid-level gossip fodder, at the time of her first steps out into the world again after sustaining multiple losses must have been awful.

The very next day, Patti made a surprise appearance on the second stage at Lollapalooza on Randall's Island in New York City. Jay Dee Daugherty was friends with the alternative music festival's tour director, Stuart Ross, and had called him for passes. Ross replied, "Ask Patti if she wants to play the second stage." Jay Dee called him back an hour later and said that she would do it.[6] When the set was over, an old friend found what they insisted was the only payphone on Randall's Island, called me, and screamed that they had just seen Patti Smith play at Lollapalooza.

I did not believe them at first, then I was furious that I had missed it, and then I remembered she was coming to Seattle, where I had been living since earlier that year. A few hours later, a report went up on the music website *Addicted to Noise* and email began landing in my inbox from people I hadn't heard from in years. They were either at the performance or had heard about it and wanted to share their excitement with me. That unplanned Lollapalooza appearance seemed to signal to the faithful that this was not going to be a rare thing. It sure *felt* like Patti Smith was back out in the music world and playing concerts with regularity.

Over Labor Day, Patti was scheduled to appear with Jim Carroll at the Seattle arts festival Bumbershoot. A few days before it kicked off, I got an email from a local poet friend saying that Patti was going to do a surprise performance in the afternoon before her appearance with Jim Carroll later that night at the Opera House. She told me that I could tell friends but asked me to please not put it on the internet. I arrived early enough to secure a spot up front, along with a few dozen others who had been tipped off and were standing around trying to act extremely casual while hoping that our intel was correct. No one even wanted to talk about it, but there were many hopeful and knowing smiles.

And then Patti goddamned Smith walked onstage, wearing a plain white T-shirt and jeans and her hair in braids, accompanied by Tony Shanahan on acoustic guitar. "Sixteen and time to pay off," she began, that first line, that groundbreaking, heart-stopping first line. I never got to hear her read "Piss Factory," and I am surrounded by people who either never got to hear Patti Smith's voice live or thought they would never hear it again. We are alive and the sky is blue and we are standing together in a place where we get to see and hear and feel it happen together as opposed to listening to it in our cars or our bedrooms. I do not remember much beyond a mixture of shock and joy. Later, she presented a different set of songs and poems over in the Opera House; it wasn't packed, probably because it was scheduled against the Ramones, but the air vibrated with excitement from the crowd's energy. Patti Smith! And Jim Carroll! Seattle was still cool in 1995, but it would never be *Patti and Jim at the Chelsea* cool.

Patti sat in the lobby after the show signing copies of *Early Work*, and every cool person in Seattle who would never wait on a line for anything patiently queued up. I don't know what I said, if anything; I just remember her sitting there with a huge smile, and I walked away realizing that I had just said "Hello" or "Thank you" or something inane to *Patti Smith*. It is clichéd to say something like "I have waited my whole life for this moment," but clichés are clichés because they are true. I honestly had never thought this day would happen. But it did.

For years, we had defended her work and her influence. We had played her on our college radio shows, included her songs on mix tapes and then mix CDs we made for friends or new lovers, watched new artists clearly influenced by her arrive on the scene. In the years she had been in Michigan, her influence and estimation had only grown. And now we would all get to see where she would pick up her art and what she would do next.

"Can ya believe it, Ma? I'm gonna play with Bob!" Patti says, giggling and doing a jig like a football player's dance in the end zone.[7] Later that year, Patti was asked to open for Bob Dylan on his Paradise Lost tour in December 1995. "What I gleaned from Bob is that he felt it would be good for me to come back out, that he thought people should see me," she told Ben Edmonds in *Mojo*. "I wouldn't presume to speak for him, but he has been so highly influential that he knows probably what it tasted like to be influential and then get shuffled around somewhere. I guess he felt I could use some encouragement."[8]

There was, of course, the minor matter of her not having a touring band. But she assembled the musicians with whom she had been in the studio recording *Gone Again*: Lenny Kaye, Jay Dee Daugherty, Tony Shanahan, Tom Verlaine, and newcomer Oliver Ray. "I wanted to do it so badly that we prepared ourselves practically on stage," Patti said. "I think we had about five hours of rehearsal. But all of us had pretty much played together, and we all pooled the things we could do."[9]

Dylan has never made a statement about inviting Patti

to join him on this tour, so I'm guessing about his motivations. He knew that he was extending a meaningful offer, sharing not only his stage but also introducing, or reintroducing, her to his audience. He also knew that no matter how nervous or unsure she was about going on the road, she wouldn't say no to him. But the most important thing? "Because they were very local [shows] I could easily take my kids or just be away for a night, so I decided to do that," she explained to a journalist.[10]

Then Dylan challenged her even further by asking Patti to choose a song for the two of them to perform together. "So I looked through his lyric book, and I realized what a profound opportunity this was," she remembered. "This was somebody that I had adored and admired since I was 15 years old, giving me the opportunity to sing any one of his songs with him."[11] She chose "Dark Eyes," a song from his 1985 album *Empire Burlesque*. Even though he had performed the song only once before, ten years earlier in Australia, Bob said yes.

Patti said she selected "Dark Eyes" because it wasn't as well known, she liked the lyrics, and it was a good song for her voice — she had been doing an acoustic version at a few of her shows. "It would have been very obvious to do 'Highway 61' or something, or 'Like a Rolling Stone.' It would have been fun, but I wanted to experience doing something beautiful with him. And it was beautiful."[12]

They first performed the duet at the Orpheum Theater in Boston. When they finished, Bob said, "A lot of girls have come along since Patti started, but Patti's still the best, you know." Then he kissed her. "I truthfully wasn't certain how I would be received, or what I should do, and being encouraged by him was very important to me," she said. "He was very encouraging to me about my place in the community of rock 'n' roll."[13] In Boston, Patti seemed to be in shock as she left the stage to a standing ovation. But as the tour progressed, the emotional dynamic between the two of them expanded, as did her self-confidence. By the time she reached the last shows in Philadelphia, her presence was more comfortable and self-assured, less an acolyte than an equal.

During the tour, various male members of the Bob Dylan community would report on the shows in internet forums. They were, for the most part, supportive and complimentary of the musical performance, which was a stunning moment to witness, both emotionally and musically. However, more than a few correspondents tried to respectfully (or not so respectfully) imply that something else was going on between the pair beyond their professional collaboration.

At the time, I angrily wrote the gossip off as the jealous mumblings of Dylan purists until I saw video of various appearances, and the only correction I had to offer (and likely did somewhere on Usenet) was that the vibe was obviously mutual and that the tired, outdated, and sexist trope that pursued her through the 1970s — that she was an opportunist and one step above a groupie — was clearly making a comeback. It doesn't even matter if you are Patti Smith, you're going to have to fight to prove you belong. Despite the years that had passed, we had not made much progress at all.

The Dylan outing would play a key role in the completion of *Gone Again*. Working on a record that was supposed to be the next one she made with Fred was emotionally challenging. "We were 80 percent done with the record and I had to stop," she told Edmonds. "But I got a lot of energy and positive feelings from the Dylan experience, and then we went in and completed the album. Those dates gave me my confidence back."[14]

Patti and the kids spent the summer back in New York City living in a townhouse loaned by friends while she worked on her next album. She had returned once again to Electric Lady, at Lenny's suggestion. "It's right on 8th Street, so you can walk out at three in the morning and there are people on the streets. It's a good energy," she told Edmonds.[15] She was coming back to where it all started with the "Piss Factory" single, and then *Horses*, allowing herself to just exist in the city, being able to walk everywhere again. Even if the city had changed since she had left, there were still her old familiar songlines, those paths across the city where you can see the ghosts of the buildings and the people and the energy that was there before. And to be back at Electric Lady Studios, the house that Jimi built,[16] was nothing short of a living ouroboros.[17]

"I was standing by myself in the hallway looking at those murals, when I remembered standing in that same spot in 1975 and Robert Mapplethorpe taking a picture of me and John Cale," she told Edmonds. "Lenny came out and stood next to me and said, 'Amazing, isn't it?' It was like he could feel what I was feeling."[18]

Patti had started thinking about her next record as early as March 1995. She had conversations with Lenny about the songs she had written and outlined her vision for the album. "It was all going to be very acoustic, almost Appalachian in style," Lenny told *Addicted to Noise*. "The last thing Fred did was teach her chords and it was interesting to me that what she did with her grief was sit down and play guitar for literally six to eight hours a day, using these chords."[19]

Even in her grief, she was still *working*. She was letting the work comfort her and give her strength. In the end, she wrote three-quarters of the music on *Gone Again*, something she had never done. In Patti's mind, she was still following the plan she and Fred had made. "We were going to record this summer. We were going to get some people together, I know who he wanted," she told *Addicted to Noise*. "He really wanted to become more active again. We had to for various reasons. Because we had things to say, and also for practical reasons. As parents we had to get back to work again because we had to start thinking about Jack and Jesse's future. So we had our game plan, and so I was already primed towards certain things."[20]

The songs evolved as Patti eased her way back into live performance, and she discovered that stepping back on-stage was different from what she thought it would be. "I imagined that I had changed quite a bit, becoming a wife and mother and withdrawing from public life for so long that I would be a lot quieter on stage," she told *Addicted to Noise*. "I imagined that I would just be sort of straightforward and dignified and somewhat folky. And I was kind of amazed to find that [that's not the case]. I'm still ready to kick a photographer in the face."[21]

Gone Again, released in June 1996, is a triumph on all levels. You hear and feel Patti's sorrow, her anger, her determination, her relief. There are remarkable moments as well as one of the finest songs ("Beneath the Southern Cross") in her entire catalog. For someone who said she had only kept up with recent music by what she heard on the radio, the music sounds fresh. Some of that is attributable to Lenny's work as a producer in the post-PSG years, but the rest was mostly kismet — Patti wrote her songs using the chords that she knew, the chords that Fred had taught her. Working within this simple chord structure unintentionally put Patti's new music adjacent to post-punk and grunge. Her declamatory, electric singing style, the element she was certain would no longer be a part of her live persona, was still very much there and would sound familiar to anyone listening to an "alternative" radio station with an *X* in the call letters.

The album's strongest tracks are the ones she is still performing, almost three decades after they were written. "About a Boy," written in response to Kurt Cobain's suicide, is about death, about excess, about chaos. The anguish manifests itself both in the lyrics and in the accompaniment, the shimmering, dive-bombing guitars (courtesy of Oliver Ray) that feel like a human voice wailing in grief. It is angry, but it is alive. "Wing" is a simple, timeless ballad that Patti fills with the strength of her vocal delivery, and its emotional impact shifts from mournful to playful based on the context of the performance.

And then there's "Beneath the Southern Cross," which I'll hold up against any of her songs from any era as one of her finest and most essential pieces of work. The studio version is magnificent, but it is in live performance where the song expands into its fullest potential; it is ecstatic and wide-ranging and never sounds the same twice. It is exactly the kind of ever-evolving, fluid composition she strove to write in the '70s, and I feel blessed every time I get to hear it. It is also not some Grateful Dead–like space jam; there is focus and structure and intent.

The record includes a delightful cover of Dylan's "Wicked Messenger," kind of like a souvenir T-shirt from their brief outing together, and in case you thought that in this phase of her career she might be done with large-scale improvisational pieces, there is "Fireflies," which seems related to her childhood memories of watching the woolgatherers from her bedroom window, a subject she wrote about in *Woolgathering*. The song is a walking meditation, mystical, with a touch of the shaman-raising energy. She counts her steps (a line that came from Oliver Ray), she is speaking to the dead, she is describing deep and abiding grief, doing all this while Tom Verlaine's guitar brings the picture to life.

Finally, there's "Summer Cannibals," a song that Fred had written years earlier and that Lenny painstakingly constructed from random bits of melody they found on cassettes around the house. Fred had told Patti what had inspired the song originally and she took it from there: a story about being in Atlanta with the MC5, getting invited to a decadent party, and feeling by the end of it that "they were trying to steal his soul from him," Lenny remembered.[22]

Gone Again was more than her fans could have hoped for. When artists return after a long break, they often attempt to re-create what worked before or follow the advice of well-meaning collaborators to sound more "relevant." But Patti didn't do that. *Gone Again* was a record of this artist here and now, and what she had to say was strong, multidimensional, and highly engaging.

The general tenor of the reviews of *Gone Again* was positive: they talked about her early work, explained where Patti had been and why, and then worked to contextualize the new songs. Lots of "Godmother of Punk Rock" and headlines about "return" and "resurrection." Americans are so uncomfortable with death and mourning, and we get squirmy when we have to face someone else's loss, which explains some of the critical reaction to the album. But in some ways it felt like, once again, Patti wasn't conforming to someone's expectations, and she was being evaluated on her failure to do that instead of on the album's merits.

James Wolcott, a veteran of the downtown NYC scene in the 1970s who wrote the *Village Voice* story about when Patti met Dylan, said, "At the risk of being offensive, I think she's overdoing her widowhood."[23] He later dismissed the backlash he (rightly) received for that statement by saying "It isn't as a singer-songwriter that she signifies anymore. It is as a living tarot card icon that Patti has achieved cultural ubiquity over the last two decades."[24] By relegating her to the status of crone ("living tarot card," as he put it), Wolcott is wielding that common tool of misogyny, "the dead weight of institutionalized ageism," as Vivien Goldman described it in her feminist music history, *Revenge of the She-Punks*.[25]

As another writer noted (in an otherwise brutal dismissal of her entire career), "When, several years back, Eric Clapton milked his son's death for a song, the record-buying public, not to mention the industry, seemed in no big hurry to remind him of the dignity of private suffering."[26]

"You're only allowed a small bit of sainthood," Patti told *Addicted to Noise* in June. "They'll be after me soon enough. . . . The press and everybody, I promise you, will be turning on me soon."[27]

*   *   *

For someone who stated that she would never again tour to any serious extent, Patti's 1996 touring schedule was ambitious, with dates in both the United States and abroad organized around the children's school schedule, television appearances, benefit concerts, support slots, and literary events.

This was a *tour*. It was not a ceremonial outing, but very much an artist hitting the road in support of a new release. If the record didn't succeed, it wouldn't be for lack of promotion. *Gone Again* peaked at number 55 on the *Billboard* 200, which, for an artist who had been out of the spotlight for as many years as she had and had occupied a niche position to begin with, was respectable.

The same band lineup that went out on the Dylan tour was in place for the 1996 tour, and the setlist was a healthy mix of new material and catalog favorites. There was a solo spot for Lenny just like old times, which would give Patti a chance to catch her breath. The tour concentrated on obvious strongholds, places where Patti had always had a strong following outside of New York—Boston, the Bay Area, Southern California—and also headed across the Atlantic where, in addition to various headlining appearances, she would begin her relationship with the European summer festival circuit. Like many American musicians, Patti would soon discover how much more hospitable, humane, and lucrative a summer performing in Europe could be. She also found that overseas, she had both her older following but also new generations who were aware of her music and wanted to see her perform. This was also the case in the United States, but on a much smaller scale than in Europe and, later, in South America and Australia.

In 1996, Patti Smith moved back to New York City permanently, buying a townhouse on the southwestern edge of Greenwich Village. If you've watched any of her live Instagram broadcasts, you've gotten a peek inside. At the time of the move, her son, Jackson, was fourteen, and her daughter, Jesse, was nine.

In 1995, an interviewer asked if the kids knew about Patti's early work, to which she responded, "The work is not appropriate for them and quite truthfully, they're not that interested. My son's more interested in Metallica and Green Day and my little girl is interested in her stuffed animals. I'm mommy to them."[28] In fact, the Smith children grew up without any knowledge of their parents' music careers; Jackson didn't find out until Fred's MC5 bandmates introduced themselves to him at his father's memorial service.

In 2018, Jackson told a journalist, "Right after he died I see in the newspapers 'Rock 'n' roll legend passes....' And I go, wait a second, is there a little more to Mommy and Daddy playing music than I knew? [laughs] There most certainly was!"[29] Jesse, being younger, understood even less. She once told an interviewer about the time in elementary school when she got an assignment where she had to write about her mother's job. "I remember sitting there and having no idea," she said. "I asked my mom and she said to write that she was a singer. Having never heard her sing before, I found this a little bit strange."[30] She remembered seeing her father's picture on MTV after his death and thinking it was because the announcer was a friend of the family.

Jackson picked up the guitar just as Patti came back to live performance and, unsurprisingly, had an instant aptitude. Lenny and the band coached him through "Smoke on the Water," and he would come out during the encores; he also admitted to yelling "Don't play it!" at shows as his mother would introduce "The Jackson Song," the *Dream of Life* track written for him. Jackson plays in many local Detroit-area bands and became a regular in his mother's band around 2007. He currently works as a real estate agent in Detroit.

"When I play with Jack, I remember truly what it tasted like to play with Fred," Patti said in the *Dream of Life* documentary.[31] Sometimes I think about how remarkable it is that she's willing to share that memory with us.

Jesse began taking piano lessons at thirteen, and around the age of sixteen, she would occasionally perform onstage with her mom. In 2003, she joined Patti in the studio to accompany her on the title track from *Trampin'*, a song that the contralto Marian Anderson sang on the steps of the Washington Memorial in April 1939. Jesse also often guests with her mom and the band onstage, but her focus is on climate activism as part of her nonprofit organization, Pathway to Paris.

Oliver Ray, whom Patti met at the reading with Allen Ginsberg in Ann Arbor in '95, joined the Smith household at some point. Oliver and Patti had begun a working partnership that transitioned into something deeper; he wrote songs with Patti, starting with "Fireflies" on *Gone Again*, and became part of her touring band, despite only having picked up the guitar a few years earlier. "I like to listen to the way he hears things" is how Lenny Kaye described him when he first joined the band. "He gives us his youthful sense of sponging, the way he takes in stuff and we see him grow every day."[32]

As a fan and critical observer of Patti Smith's work, my opinion on her relationship with Oliver Ray boils down to caring about his impact on the music. One of my all-time favorite Patti Smith songs ever, "Beneath the Southern Cross," was inspired by an experience Oliver had in the jungles of South America, so I'm pretty much okay with him. I know Lenny liked having three guitar players in the band when Oliver was around (even though Oliver maintained the sound engineer would sometimes cut him out of the mix); I am more of a rock and roll purist and like fewer people in my rock bands, but I didn't think he detracted from the overall experience of a Patti Smith show.

It's not that I am some higher being who is above

gossip—and there was definitely some about the relation-ship between Patti and Oliver, some oblique and some direct—but I'm going to base any opinion I have on what I see and hear. Patti regards him highly; he collaborated with her for almost a decade; she continues to promote his work and invite him to open for her shows; he was the basis for one of the characters in *Year of the Monkey*. If anything, I wish sometimes that I had her incredible ability to maintain long-standing friendships with people with whom she was once romantically involved. In 2020, she told the podcaster Marc Maron, when discussing her friendship with Sam Shepard, "We had a great trust and great communication and a friendship that we had, and the aspects of that working relationship and that trust were way more important than you know, a romantic relationship, if that's not what you're destined to have."[33] It would be better for everybody if we all had this skill.

On Valentine's Day 1997, Patti and the band were the musical guests on the *Late Show with David Letterman*, performing their newly retooled version of Bo Diddley's "Who Do You Love?"—imagine, if you will, that the Ramones had covered the song, but took creative liberties with the lyrics to turn it into an anthem about environmental awareness where the beloved is Mother Earth.

The appearance was ostensibly to promote the annual Tibet House benefit the following week, but outside New

York City it felt like a signal being transmitted from another country. Wearing her *Horses* ensemble, she was energetic and sounded fantastic, and the band was in sharp sync with her and one another. Here was Patti Smith on late-night television, something that just happens on a Friday night when you're brushing your teeth and getting ready for bed. By 1997, with the release of her second post-Michigan album, *peace and noise*, it felt like this was a thing you could start to count on being there, that, goddess willing, Patti was here to stay with us.

And she was. Fitting work in around the children's school schedule until they graduated, she would become a regular at Philip Glass's Tibet House benefit concerts, would soon commence her yearly duo (and later trio) of shows at Bowery Ballroom at the end of the year, and would be invited to participate in literary festivals and events around the world. One year I got a call from a friend in New York who was watching the NYC Village Halloween Parade on television who said, "You're not going to believe who's on a float on the corner of West Eighth and Sixth Avenue, playing 'People Have the Power.' "

There were readings at the main branch of the New York Public Library, yearly events at the Metropolitan Museum of Art, a reading at the annual lecture of the Blake Society, a support slot with U2 when they played Madison Square Garden, guest appearances at R.E.M. concerts, and a regular calendar of tours and live appearances, both in the United States and abroad. It was all kinds of amazing and surreal, and not just for fans and admirers of her music. Lenny said, "What really amazes me most about this Patti thing is that it seems to have kind of entered the continuum. It's almost like in science fiction where they do the light year thing, where they fold space and come out."[34] For her part, Patti appeared energized and positive. She was always a phenomenal interview—unless she was asked shallow questions, and even then she answered with gravity and genuine intent.

The sorties out on "jobs," as she has always referred to performances, weren't just ways to make money (though that was part of it; this is her profession after all). There is part of Patti that wants to be out on the road, in the spirit of the wandering troubadour. She is coming to your town to bring you the news, tell you some stories, to sing you her latest songs plus some old ones that sparked a memory and new ones that caught her ear (I am thinking of the time on her birthday in 2013 when she launched into a cover of Rihanna's "Stay" at Webster Hall in New York City). Even without any new records, if Patti Smith had only chosen to come and say hello annually, doing short tours, festivals, and benefits, she would still be adding more to the culture than most people do in a lifetime.

And then there was the work she did beyond music, the most successful and well-known being *Just Kids*, her 2010 memoir of her life with Robert Mapplethorpe. But she also regularly produced essays and introductions to books by friends or artists she believed in, poetry collections, and then two more memoirs, *M Train* and *Year of the Monkey*, after *Just Kids*. Add to that her work as a visual artist, whether it was the mixed-media retrospectives at the Robert Miller Gallery in New York City, her photography exhibits at the Fondation Cartier pour l'art contemporain in Paris, or her solo show at the Wadsworth Atheneum in Hartford, Connecticut.

Patti Smith works harder and more consistently than most people realize unless you are paying close attention — and even if you are, you will likely be overwhelmed by the sheer volume of her output. It is inspiring to watch her work as much as she does, and it is heartening that she is not coy about her process: she does not pretend that it is easy or that the Muses magically descend from the sky. It's not that she demystifies the process. It's that she refuses to mystify it at all. Obviously, she has been gifted with tremendous talent, but no one would know about it if she wasn't working. She is holding herself, and us, to a high standard.

Patti reentered the traditional music business right before file sharing, as the alternative press began to splinter apart, FM radio became more and more regimented, and record sales moved from physical to digital outlets. Basically, none of the outlets that had supported her in the 1970s worked in the same way they had. She did not have a manager; in 2002, she told the *New Yorker*, "I'm pretty much unmanageable at this point." She relies on Rosemary Carroll, her attorney, to handle what needs to be handled, and so Patti has had to learn how to navigate the new aspects of this world she once again inhabited.

She goes off on a hilarious rant during one of the album release shows at CBGB for *peace and noise* in 1997, complaining that the album's single, "1959," was being released as a "radio-only" single: "Before, they just, like, put the singles in the stores, and then you bought one, or didn't buy it!" She then veers off, opining on commercial radio, college radio, the *Billboard* charts, and Camden, New Jersey. Patti explains what the song is about to the person in the audience who interrupted her stream of consciousness to ask. "Why do you let lame people run the radio stations?" Patti asks before declaring, "See if the radio's playing it, and if they're not, report back to me!" The field marshal had spoken, her half-serious command not unlike a request in the first fan club zine in May 1976. Under the headline "You Can Help," the notice requests: "Continue to contact your area radio stations requesting Patti's current single 'Gloria.' You can also write to the producers of the 'NBC Saturday Night' show telling them how much you enjoyed Patti's performance on the show."[35]

Patti's records have never been huge commercial sellers, and she has never had a gold record, which, as determined by the Recording Industry Association of America (RIAA), signifies 500,000 units sold. In 2002, the *New Yorker* noted that it was generally believed *Horses* had sold 350,000 copies by that point.[36] For a work that consistently ranks highly in "Best Albums of All Time"–type lists, that figure seems low. *Horses* was ranked twenty-sixth on *Rolling Stone*'s "500 Greatest Albums of All Time" and seventh on NPR's "The 150 Greatest Albums Made by Women."[37] Carole King's *Tapestry*, released in 1971, ranks right above *Horses* on the *Rolling Stone* list and went gold right after it came out, but then took another twenty-plus years to go platinum (which signals a million units sold). Considering that tracks from *Tapestry* were on the radio approximately every five minutes in the '70s on both AM and FM—my mother had the 8-track, and her tastes ran more toward Barbra Streisand—it should have sold more than it did.

I would like to pause and interrogate the fact that my first instinct when confronted with this data was to look at Patti's work compared to that of other women—and not, say, to the Velvet Underground and Nico (whose eponymous debut ranked twenty-third on the *Rolling Stone* list), Bob Dylan (*Highway 61 Revisited*, #18), or the Clash (*London Calling*, #16)—and acknowledge that even someone actively working to elevate the work of women within rock and roll can be influenced by subconscious bias. The patriarchy is real.

I found that the Velvets have no RIAA certifications in the United States for their first album, but the disc went platinum in the United Kingdom (which means more than 300,000 units sold); Dylan went gold upon release in 1965 but didn't hit platinum until 1997; and the Clash's record did not go gold until a decade after its release (and that was mostly attributable to one of their songs from a *different album* being used in a Levi's Jeans commercial).[38] The one thing all these records have in common with *Horses* is that they were phenomenally influential.

But influence has rarely translated into commercial success, and there is no more convincing proof of that than Patti Smith's career. The music manager Danny Fields said in 2002, "If you could quantify the intensity of the fans' love for Patti, she would be more popular than Alanis Morissette."[39] But the reality is this remark from the woman herself the year prior: "I sort of straddle this interesting position. My band and I are struggling in an underground band but I seem to get a lot of attention. I don't know how the hell else to put it."[40]

It was remarkable that after not having put out any records in the eight years between *Dream of Life* and *Gone Again* that Patti would follow up the latter with *peace and noise* less than a year later. Lenny Kaye had noted in a 1996 interview that they had four or five songs left over from *Gone Again*, which was notable because Patti generally did not have material left over from recording sessions in the '70s.

It was also notable because once again she put out a record worth listening to; too many legacy artists who have been around for decades release music that is essentially an excuse to tour, so they can say they're not a nostalgia act, but the work doesn't hold up and the songs fall by the wayside as the tour progresses. For example, I remember being glad when I could stop pretending I liked the Rolling

Stones' 1997 *Bridges to Babylon* and accepted that I could just go see them perform without needing to twist myself into knots to emotionally invest myself in their newer music.

In an interview to promote *peace and noise*, Patti remarked, "I was strong enough to do this record, now I feel strong enough to fight for this record. Because this is definitely a record that's going to have to be fought for. *Gone Again* as a piece of work was successful. As a commercial entity it was not successful. People imagine it was successful but it wasn't."[41]

While *peace and noise* reflects her grieving process, it also shows her starting to turn outward. This meant she was writing about the passing of Allen Ginsberg and the death of Benjamin, an Atlanta musician whose work she admired, but also the Heaven's Gate cult mass suicide, the plight of the Tibetan people, and climate change. "This record is the first record I've done in a long time where all of the ideas come from my own meditations," Patti told the *Philadelphia City Paper*.[42]

My favorite track is "Dead City," a lament about Detroit, though it could be any decaying but once great city. It's loud and raucous, with super crunchy guitars. I am also a big fan of the masterpiece of noise known as "Spell," which sets Allen Ginsberg's "Footnote to Howl" over resonant, dirgelike music composed by Oliver Ray. On the album, it is controlled and meditative; live, it is another number, in which the assemblage of musicians holds forth based on the energy Patti sets out, which she then grabs control of when she breaks out her clarinet at the end in what the great poet himself would probably call "bop kabbalah."[43]

She performed it with the band at the 1998 memorial service for Allen held at the Cathedral of St. John the Divine, and it was both sacred and profane and just flat-out ecstatic. Patti dropped the book she was reading from, picked up her clarinet, and wailed, absolutely going for it, with the sound of her instrument echoing up to the cathedral's vaulted roof. The degree to which she continued to throw herself into improvisation, especially at that point in her career, is exemplary. It requires so much discipline, as well as willingness to fail. Most rock and roll artists in their fifties are falling back on their body of work and not walking onstage and risking falling flat on their face.

The other big improv number is "Memento Mori," which in Latin means "remember death." Within the song, Patti vibes on a story about the last hours of Blind Lemon Jefferson and then urges the track into swinging from calm chanting to frenzy: "We remember / everything," she intones toward the end. *Everything*. It is the shortest 10:34 song you will ever hear because there is always something happening, and you will hear something different every time you listen to it.

"I'm not interested, especially at this time in my life, in being a cult hero or an obscure artist," she told *Addicted to*

Noise after the release of *peace and noise*. "I do this kind of work because I think I have important things to communicate. I believe in my band. I want people to hear it."[44]

Along with that tenacious statement came *Gung Ho* in 2000, the last studio album under her contract with Arista. *Gung Ho* is thematically a continuation of the direction Patti set for herself upon her return. She is concerned with the state of the planet, she wants to inspire people to do good things, she wants to push civilization in a positive direction. The record touches on Mother Teresa, Jerry Garcia, political involvement, environmental activism, commercialism, as well as simple storytelling for its own sake.

"New Party," a raucous and delightfully rhythmic call to arms, was adopted as the official anthem for activist Ralph Nader's 2000 presidential campaign. Patti appeared in support of Nader at multiple benefits and rallies, and she took a lot of heat in various places for her support of a third party candidate. But she was using her platform for a cause she believed in, and her position remained consistent. "He's an honest man," she told the *New Yorker*. "He has a code and he lives by it. He's committed to justice for the common man. He's as committed to his work as Blake or Genet were to theirs."[45]

"Glitter in Their Eyes" was an unlikely single, as it features lyrics about materialism and the World Trade Organization, but you can dance to it and there's a guitar solo from Tom Verlaine. The song would earn Patti a Grammy nomination for Best Female Rock Vocal Performance, which, unfortunately, she would lose to Sheryl Crow. "Grateful" was inspired by the ghost of Jerry Garcia, and "Lo and Beholden" is melodically and energetically related to "Ain't It Strange" from *Radio Ethiopia*. The grand improvisational number on *Gung Ho* was the title track, based on the life of Hồ Chí Minh; I always appreciate the effort but have never felt like this number gelled.

The cadence of new album releases slowed down after 2000. Writing is the part of the process that takes Patti the longest time, and in this particular decade, she was working on *Just Kids* and focusing more on visual art. She was still touring, as that was her primary income generator, but there wouldn't be a new record until *Trampin'* in 2004.

That album was not her strongest work in this post-'95 period. It sounds great and the individual songs are well written; however, it doesn't feel as cohesive a collection of music compared to its three predecessors. Furthermore, with a few exceptions, it is challenging to discern the messages being communicated by the lyrics; they simply don't have the strength or specificity that characterizes the majority of Patti's other work.

"Peaceable Kingdom" and "My Blakean Year" are the standout tracks. With "Peaceable Kingdom," the music is in her best range and the message of unity and a sadness about its absence is clear, even without knowing the song was written for the American peace activist Rachel Corrie, who was crushed to death by an Israeli army bulldozer while protesting the demolition of Palestinian homes. It is a beautiful moment. "My Blakean Year" chronicles how William Blake was virtually unknown in his lifetime but still worked hard. Patti wrote both the words and the music, and if there's an event at which Patti is making an appearance and there is a guitar onstage, chances are you are going to hear "My Blakean Year" — it has become one of her most-performed songs.

The 2012 *Banga* is a solid, expansive collection of songs and a cohesive listening experience drawn from far-out and far-flung influences: the stories of Nikolai Gogol, the life of St. Francis, Mikhail Bulgakov's novel *The Master and Margarita*, Sun Ra, a girl group eulogy in honor of Amy Winehouse ("This Is the Girl"), the Russian filmmaker Andrei Tarkovsky, the Tōhoku earthquake in Japan, the recently deceased actress Maria Schneider, explorer Amerigo Vespucci (and explorers in general), and a spellbinding cover of Neil Young's "After the Goldrush."

The most disappointing release from this period is the 2007 *Twelve*, an album of cover songs. The inclusion of some tracks are blindingly obvious — Jimi's "Are You Experienced?"; Neil's "Helpless"; the Stones' "Gimme Shelter"; Dylan's "Changing of the Guards"; even the Jefferson Airplane's "White Rabbit" doesn't feel too far off the mark. But the songs chosen for this record were all newly selected, not songs that the band already had a relationship with, and without that cumulative emotional connection, they fall somewhat flat. Overall, *Twelve* feels extremely anticlimactic to be the record that follows Patti's induction into the Rock & Roll Hall of Fame earlier that year. A live album—something that's been promised for years but always seems to stall out—would have been far more representative of her influence and body of work.

In 2016, Patti began to work with the experimental sound group Soundwalk Collective, supplying the vocals for *Killer Road*, a soundscape about the last day of German singer Nico's life. Nico, of course, sang four songs on the Velvet Underground's debut album, which ensured her place in history, but she struggled with drug addiction and remained a cult figure. Nico died in 1988 as the result of inadequate care following a bicycle accident, and *Killer Road* has Patti reading unpublished songs of Nico's over a collection of sounds generated by the collective. Patti's daughter, Jesse, also participated. I saw its only performance and had nightmares afterward, which, in this context, seems like a success for the collective.

In 2019 and 2020, Patti would continue to collaborate with Soundwalk Collective on a collection of projects grouped under the name "Perfect Version": *The Peyote Dance*, *Mummer Love*, and *Peradam*. Each centered around a writer—Antonin Artaud, Arthur Rimbaud, and René Daumal, respectively—and specifically on how each of the artists felt a strong drive to travel in order to bring new perspectives to their work. Patti reads the work of the respective poets, and the collective builds an immersive soundtrack that incorporates instrumentals and field recordings. If this sounds like "Radio Ethiopia" taken to its logical conclusion, that would be an accurate description, and I love that she continues to explore the outer edges of sound when given the opportunity.

One Halloween when I was in college, I had no energy for a costume, so I went for the easiest thing I could: narrow black jeans from Reminiscence (a critical location for this item of clothing at the time), men's white button-down shirt, black suit jacket, and, since it was the '80s, a skinny black tie. I walked into the local student hangout and most of the people gave me a hard time for not having a costume, while my friends rolled their eyes and said, "Really, you're going to just dress like Patti on the cover of *Horses*? How obvious, try harder next time."

Patti's image on that record is indelible, as was the rest of her '70s ensemble. We all wanted those perfect Ray-Ban sunglasses, even if she admits she stole the look from Dylan. I tried in vain for years to master the haircut, begging hairdressers to give me "a cross between Keith Richards and Patti Smith" with mixed degrees of success. I wore oversized blazers not because of *Annie Hall* but because I saw Patti in *CREEM* wearing one. We wanted to look cool, so we tried to copy her. She wanted to look cool, so she copied Bob Dylan. It is a rock and roll story as old as time.

It was charming to see that the "*Horses* couture" (as I have always referred to it) was omnipresent on special occasions as Patti moved forward in her art and public life. But the area in which she has had the most sartorial impact these days is what myself and other women of a certain aesthetic like to refer to as "the uniform": a T-shirt, usually from Electric Lady; jeans, rolled up; boots, either lace-up or slip-on (she mentioned onstage that she had switched boots so she didn't have to constantly unlace them for security while on tour); and a black jacket, which would hold her glasses, pens, a notebook, sometimes a paperback. She developed a particular fondness for a certain type of cotton lisle socks from Japan (by the design house Antipast), which she colloquially refers to as "bee socks." (One year at her annual birthday show, when the band gave her multiple pairs as a gift,[46] she exclaimed onstage, "Four pairs of bee socks!" and waved them at the audience.)

The jacket she wore most of the time was a gift from the Belgian designer Ann Demeulemeester, a member of the Antwerp Six fashion collective, whose radical style was widely recognized as being influenced by punk rock. So, it wasn't a huge surprise that Demeulemeester was an avid fan and, after Fred Smith's passing, sent a box of her white button-down shirts to Detroit as both thanks and consolation. In the introduction to an eponymous monograph chronicling Demeulemeester's career, Patti writes, "This modest gesture produced the joy of recognition. I understood that I was not alone."[47] This collaboration would further manifest itself in Demeulemeester's 1998 spring ready-to-wear collection, which she told *Vogue* was directly inspired by Patti's use of Allen Ginsberg's "Footnote to Howl" in *peace and noise*'s "Spell." And one of the jackets, which Patti wore "until it was completely broken," said Demeulemeester, is now in the Rock & Roll Hall of Fame.[48]

When the *New Yorker* interviewed Georgia O'Keefe in 1929, she said she wore black because "if she started picking out colors for dresses, she would not have time for painting."[49] When I read this quote in the Brooklyn Museum retrospective of O'Keefe's work, the first person I thought of was Patti Smith.

These days, "the uniform" is freeing Patti in the same way it did O'Keefe, and the same concept is what allowed Elizabeth Warren to get dressed in four minutes while on the campaign trail—it eliminates decision fatigue.[50] Simplifying one's wardrobe creates space in one's life and brain for art and dreaming. It allows Patti to pack light for tour—a constant in her Instagram feed is her tiny metal Rimowa suitcase, ready for the road. "Just the stuff I need, lightweight enough to wash in a hotel sink," Patti writes in an Instagram post on July 28, 2018, illustrated by photos of three T-shirts (two Electric Lady, one featuring a William Blake illustration from an Ann Demeulemeester line), a handkerchief, Weleda salt toothpaste, the infamous bee socks, her passport, and a pile of euros. It's not that she's a minimalist or eschews possessions—she is proud of owning furniture from Cafe 'Ino and the set of *Law and Order*—but traveling light is freedom and independence. She carries her own bags, which means she can change her plans at will and she doesn't have to worry about losing things on the road.

The formal *Horses* ensemble still comes out at special moments. "I had my *Horses* clothes on; I looked like Baudelaire," she told David Fricke in 1996, describing the night she went to the premiere of *Ladies and Gentlemen: The Rolling Stones* and then went down to CBGB for the first time. It was also what she chose to wear when inaugurated into the Rock & Roll Hall of Fame in 2007, and both Patti and the band would deliberately dress in black and white on the *Horses* fortieth anniversary tour in 2015. It is hers. She owns it.

As someone who came of age as second-wave feminism transitioned into third-wave feminism, I like to believe that I understand some of Patti's reluctance to identify with feminist ideology, especially in the seventies. Had she not consistently pushed her stance that she was "beyond gender," she would have had to deal with questions about bra burning and why she hates men since not wearing dresses, makeup, or high heels was viewed as subversive. Those clichés were weaponized against me even as a child in elementary school when I would speak up and demand to be allowed to do something that the boys were doing but the girls were prohibited from doing, like being allowed on the monkey bars if I was wearing a skirt or participating in extracurricular sports. Girls could play basketball only on a team that was organized and coached by parents, and we practiced and played in the evenings because during the day the gym might be needed for something important. (Title IX had just been passed and hadn't yet made it to our small town.)

I personally can forgive just about anything Patti said in the 1970s about feminism. That was still a tough era for anyone who existed outside of the established gender binary; women still couldn't wear slacks to work in those days unless their workplace was incredibly liberal. I was barely a teenager at the end of that decade and yet have far too many memories of men being inappropriate or predatory or both. I cannot even begin to imagine what it was like for her coming up before me. I also feel as though I understand Patti's thought process of not wanting to be restricted by any kind of movement and her belief that subscribing to a particular ideology was at odds with her way of being. Finally, she was out there blazing the goddamned trail for us with a machete; I didn't need her to also be ideologically perfect. She did far more to help the cause than hurt it.

But in the 1990s and later, it was difficult for me to believe she didn't understand that a statement like "I don't want to be known for my gender or my race or anything"[51] is a Platonic ideal when record labels, radio stations, and promoters were (and still are) saying things like "Oh, we're already playing Sheryl Crow, so we can't add you to our roster/playlist/festival."

And when Lilith Fair, the groundbreaking late-1990s music festival featuring an all-female talent lineup, was announced, I'm sure that Patti hated being asked about it at every opportunity. From the perspective of "You're a woman musician and this is a festival of women musicians so we need to ask you to comment on it!" it must have been maddening. But I was disappointed to hear her comments along the lines of how it was for "women performers who find it important to be known as a woman performer,"[52] and not acknowledging that it was a reaction to an industry that was still dominated by men and hostile to women.

Patti was actively back on the road in the festival's heyday, and it seems unthinkable that she wasn't invited — the festival's cofounders made it clear that they asked everybody — and two of the very popular choices for the nightly grand finale with all the performers were "Because the Night" and "Ghost Dance."[53] Patti rejecting Lilith Fair is unfortunate because it would have been great for the festival and the artists on the bill, and it would have delivered a new audience on the scale that *Just Kids* gave her, except this fanbase would have been focused on her music. It would also have been beneficial for Patti's pocketbook because the 1997 Lilith Fair outing was the top-grossing festival and the sixteenth highest-grossing concert tour that year.[54] I say this as someone who wasn't interested in the first round of Lilith Fair because it didn't rock quite hard enough for me, but still wholeheartedly believed it was a fantastic idea.

I do not think Patti is lying when she says she never felt she was discriminated against on account of her gender. But I am also confronted with the contradiction of how, when the fledgling Patti Smith Group was auditioning guitarists, it proved challenging because, in Patti's words, "almost to a man, none of them warmed up to the idea of a girl being the leader."[55] Patti would not be the first woman to decide it is better to insist you were not treated differently and you were always evaluated fairly than it is to face the repercussions of being thought of as less than because you weren't a man.

She is not in charge of fighting all our battles. I just wish she would join in on some of them when it feels like she could make a real difference.

— 5 —

BLUE STAR

The day before Robert Mapplethorpe died, he asked Patti to tell their story, and she promised she would. At the time she made that promise, she did not realize it would take her ten years to write the book that would become *Just Kids*. Her initial publication date was tied to the twentieth anniversary of Robert's death in 2009, but Smith was behind schedule and was going to miss her deadline. "I was in Tennessee touring with my band, and I had to go in the wheat fields to call my editor with a cell phone," she told *New York* magazine in 2010.[1]

Just Kids exceeded everyone's expectations, even those of us who had already been influenced by her life and work. I expected that the book would set the record straight, while sharing some good stories and key insights from that era, but absolutely no one expected it to be as monumental and deeply enjoyable as the final product turned out to be—or that it would be such a fantastic New York City book.

Patti connected the dots, provided the backstory, didn't skimp on the details, and took us all with her into the back room at Max's Kansas City and the Chelsea Hotel in the early '70s in a friendly voice. It's your cool cousin telling you about the time she snuck out to go see the Clash and got to meet the band after the show. Her prose is crystal clear and carefully written. It feels generous, welcoming, and accessible. I have read it multiple times and always find something new: let me go revisit Harry Smith's *Anthology of American Folk Music*, read one of Sam Shepard's short stories, or open up the Allen Ginsberg poetry collection to a random page. As I read, I hear Patti's voice saying "This is the era where everybody creates," from *Wave*'s "So You Want to Be (a Rock 'n' Roll Star)."

It was still surprising that *Just Kids* won the 2010 National Book Award in nonfiction: not because it wasn't worthy, but because Patti's work had never been part of the mainstream. *Just Kids* brought people into Patti Smith's work who might have previously believed that it was too "punk rock" or just not for them. It would be translated into French (*Rien que des gamins*), Spanish (*Éramos unos niños*), Russian (Просто дети), German (*Die Geschichte einer Freundschaft*), and twenty-five other languages. The readers who discovered her through the book ventured out to her concerts, and fans from the early days who thought their concertgoing days were behind them crept back into the fold.

"My (2010) book, *Just Kids*, has been my most successful thing," she told the *Detroit Free Press* in 2018. "It's not a record. I've never had a gold record in America, never sold a tremendous amount of records. *Just Kids*—a book—has really eclipsed everything else I've done."[2]

In the second year of the COVID-19 pandemic, she decided to launch an email newsletter to have more room to communicate than in her Instagram posts and also to serialize a story she had been working on. From my perspective, all I care about is that she continues to do work of any kind and share it with us. The longer that goes on, the better.

Following *Just Kids*, there was a rumor that Patti was working on a New York detective novel, but her next book, *M Train*, released five years later, was decidedly not that. The memoir is constructed from stylized vignettes that take you inside Patti Smith's thoughts and imagination, and it is, as one might expect, both fantastical and hilarious. She is a woman of a certain age whose husband is deceased and whose children are grown. She is able to fly to Japan on a whim; she can decide to overnight in London instead of just changing planes so she can watch her favorite British police procedurals; and she can fall in love with an ancient cottage in Rockaway Beach and figure out how to purchase it in a cash transaction with money she makes over the course of a summer's work.

Most notable in this book is how she navigates her life to include the people she has lost. She attends to her mourning. Grief is not a straightforward line, yet it is Patti's grief that the press again finds objectionable. We are taught that men should hide their emotions and women should not mourn in public unless they do it in a manner approved by men. There are no modern grief rituals in Western society, and we as a civilization are poorer for it. I don't believe she's trying to teach us how to grieve, but there are lessons in what she shows us about how she engages with it.

In many ways, *M Train* reminds me of what we would see in a few years in Patti's Instagram feed. She took to that platform like a digital native, sharing "self-pictures" (what she calls a selfie), photos of her kids, her cats, what she's reading or working on, and occasional videos giving us a refreshingly earnest and un-curated view into her life and work. And that, I think, is what most reviewers found problematic with *M Train*: it is a completely irony-free zone.

Other reviewers dismiss it with statements such as "Smith really is the kind of woman who talks to her cats," as though that is an insult.[3] But on the other hand, there is the estimable Michiko Kakutani of the *New York Times*, who began her review, "Patti Smith's achingly beautiful new book, 'M Train,' is a kaleidoscopic ballad about the losses dealt out by time and chance and circumstance."[4] The difference here is that Kakutani reviewed the book and the writing, while others reviewed their impression of the life of the person who wrote it.

Patti continued to pursue the melding of fantasy and reality in her next book, the 2019 *Year of the Monkey*. It is an absurd and engrossing read that sometimes feels like an homage to the surrealism employed by her beloved Haruki Murakami, the Japanese author of *The Wind-Up Bird Chronicle*. As in *M Train*, we are taken on another set of journeys within a larger journey. In my review of the book, I wrote that she "expertly navigates the edges around our willful suspension of disbelief, pushing at the corners, expanding the spaces of our imaginations."[5] The storytelling creates a world that feels much larger than the small book that contains it. What keeps it grounded are the characters, either real, imagined, or hybrid, with whom she interacts; what keeps it interesting are the ways she assigns significance and even motive to the inanimate objects she uses as markers and talismans.

Patti also returned to her poetry in the '00s with *Auguries of Innocence*. This is an underexamined volume that represents some of her strongest political work. Three poems deal with bombing raids, both current and historical. "Our Jargon Muffles the Drum" is both prose poem and stream of consciousness; it's the onrush of words, the movement that Patti creates, that makes it so devastating. "Birds of Iraq" is just as affecting, but for the opposite reason: its construction is more conventional, but the brevity of its lines drives the message home.

It's not surprising that a volume of poetry was overlooked, given that her records also tend to be overlooked, but it still makes me angry because these poems are quiet fire. Her poetic voice is not a trivial side pursuit.

Admittedly, where outside of a literary magazine is poetry considered with any seriousness? Yet, it is important.

In a 1977 *Village Voice* cover story, Robert Christgau mentioned a poet who "posited rather icily that Patti reads Rimbaud in translation."[6] But she *read* Rimbaud, and as a result, she got thousands more of us to read Rimbaud and poetry just generally. When I walked into English class in my freshman year of high school carrying a library copy of *The Drunken Boat*, I had no idea what the hell I was reading, but I wanted to at least *try*. My English teacher, who had been to Woodstock in 1969, asked me where my interest in the French poets came from, and she didn't blink an eye when I told her it was a musician. She recommended that I look for the *Anchor Anthology of French Poetry*, the same one Patti would write the introduction to upon its reissue in 2000. My high school peers didn't sneer at me because I was reading poetry in translation; my crime was reading poetry, period. (This even though the 1970s were the high point of Jim Morrison adulation, but it didn't take me long to figure out that, unlike Patti, they liked Jim because he was a dick, not because he was a good poet. Sorry, Patti Lee.) I kept at it. I am still at it. "Go Rimbaud, go Rimbaud."

One of my favorite things to do as a teenager was to put my headphones on, sit on the floor, light a candle, and listen to a favorite record over and over in order to copy the lyrics. If an album came with lyrics, I would ask my father to take it to work and make a photocopy so that I had the freedom to make notes on it, compile it with other lyrics, hang it on the wall, share it with friends who might have a copy on tape, and other uses I have long since forgotten. In some ways, it was samizdat, an underground activity that you didn't necessarily advertise widely, not because you would be arrested but because people would think that you were just weird. I understand now that these were early attempts at the very thing I do now—studying an artist's work—but at the time it felt like I was making a commitment as a fan by taking their words seriously.

There had not been a published collection of Patti Smith's lyrics until 1998, when the first of what would be a series of volumes under the title *Patti Smith: Complete* was released. It was a series because she was a living artist, which meant updated volumes would be published as new records came out. Not surprisingly, these were illustrated and annotated books full of photographs, illustrations, images, and commentary. There was always something new that you hadn't seen or read before that made acquiring the latest edition enjoyable—she didn't just change the font, add a short introduction, and say it was updated. These books remind me so much of the assemblages that populated the album inserts for *Easter* and *Wave*, which were more like collages or installations with images, commentary, poetry, and other elements deliberately displayed. They were extensions of the album artwork, the kind of precious bonuses you hoped for when you got an album home and slit the shrink-wrap.

But her work on these volumes was also a deliberate act of ownership on her part. This was before the proliferation of lyric sites on the internet, but you could find unofficial transcriptions of lyrics on Usenet and then later on random websites. Publishing the books also allowed Patti to contextualize and control how her lyrics were presented. And, finally, these collections were acts of determination: not all song lyrics are worthy of anthologizing, and not all songwriters want to publish their lyrics in this way. If the world would not extend her the recognition she deserved, she would clear a place at the table for herself, saying, in effect, "My work is important, my work is worthy of collection, the entire body of work is sufficiently meritorious to be considered." It is a woman demanding to be seen and heard, seizing her own destiny, guiding her own legacy. It is both punk rock and feminist as fuck.

After taking the second half of the 1990s to reorient her presence in rock and roll, Patti had the space to once again focus on her visual art. She had been in talks with the Andy Warhol Museum at the beginning of the '00s about curating a small exhibition of her visual work combined with artifacts like manuscripts and photographs. But this plan changed in the aftermath of 9/11, when she found herself again turning to her work to try to make sense of a tragedy that defied all logic. She began painting and drawing, reproducing one image from the ruins of the World Trade Center over and over again in different forms and approaches. She wrote, "Now I feel compelled to utter, 'I am an American artist, and I feel guilty about everything.' In spite of this I will not turn away: I will keep working."[7] These drawings became the *9/11 Babelogue*, otherwise referred to as the *9/11 Series*.

It is a profound body of work, complex, intricate, and deeply emotional. The repetition of the images feels chant-like; her printing them over and over evokes a rosary. I also see her using the art to find solace and to make sense of chaos, hatred, love, war, and devotion. She uses written script as an essential structural element, and the result is an illuminated manuscript, a poem, a song, and a prayer. The remark about being an American artist derives, of course, from "Babelogue" on *Easter*, where she declared, "I am an American artist and I feel no guilt."

In 2002, the Warhol Museum hosted the exhibition *Strange Messenger: The Work of Patti Smith*. This first-ever museum exhibition of her work surveyed her entire career as a visual artist from art school sketches made in the 1960s all the way to the entirety of the *9/11* drawings.

In the months after her husband's death, Patti turned to her artistic practice, as she always had, to provide her with a sense of consolation and meaning, only to find that she didn't have the focus to pursue any of her usual mediums. So, she began taking Polaroid photographs; the simplicity and immediacy of the instant photograph made her feel a sense of completion and accomplishment. This direction would eventually lead to her solo photographic exhibition, *Patti Smith: Camera Solo*, at Hartford's Wadsworth Atheneum in 2011.

A set of her Polaroids would also become part of the multimedia *Land 250* exhibition in 2008 at the Fondation Cartier pour l'art contemporain in Paris. This was her first major exhibition in Europe to focus on the entirety of her visual art from 1967 to the present, and the show's catalog focused on her photography, making it the first formal collection of her photographic work (and to date it still is the largest such volume).

The book contains more than two hundred images, including 1969 photographs of Robert Mapplethorpe's hands at work; images from her travels; photographs of her children, including one of Jackson with the tattoo of his father's image on his shoulder; grave markers; statuary; artifacts; photos from her trip with Fred to French Guiana, which would be memorialized in *M Train*; and much more. The curation of the sequencing of images in the book is deliberate but subtle; it seems to be guided more by a feeling than a hard concept, but the result is that it gently motivates you to keep turning the pages.

Nowadays, we get to see her photographic eye in her Instagram feed, a more instantly gratifying approach for both the viewer and the photographer. I have always suspected that Patti took to Instagram so quickly because the size limitations of the square were reminiscent of the space in a developed Polaroid and because the immediacy of both the image and public reaction to it were gently addictive.

All the exhibitions are about Patti Smith assuming the gravity and respect she is entitled to as an artist, but which she might not receive without taking the initiative to make sure she is recognized and counted.

While Patti needed to explicitly claim her place within the American music scene, her fans in the United Kingdom did not need any reminders. In 2005, she was invited to curate the Meltdown Festival at the South Bank Centre in London, two weeks of performances directed by an artist of cultural importance. Previous curators of the festival included David Bowie, Laurie Anderson, and Yoko Ono; the *Guardian* reported that Patti promised, in typical work-centric fashion, "I'll perform myself, but if anyone else needs a bit of backing vocal, clarinet or a shirt ironed, I'll be there."[8]

Almost all the performers she invited to be part of the festival agreed to appear, which constituted a diverse list including Yoko Ono, Marianne Faithfull, Sinéad O'Connor, Billy Bragg, Steve Earle, Jeff Beck, Johnny Marr, and Kristin Hersh, as well as old friends John Cale, Television, Mick Jones of the Clash (in his new outfit Carbon/Silicon), and Carolyn Striho (from Detroit Energy Asylum, the band that rehearsed with Patti to reacclimate her to live performance in 1995). By the end of the festival, the *Guardian* declared, "Patti Smith's stewardship of Meltdown . . . will stand as one of the most eclectic of the festival's history."[9]

The 2005 Meltdown was the first time Patti and the band performed *Horses* in its entirety.[10] That evening, which was widely regarded as the highlight of the festival, sold out at once. But the second most-anticipated evening was the performance of *The Coral Sea*, which featured Patti backed by Kevin Shields of My Bloody Valentine. Everyone told Patti she would never get him to agree to perform; MBV hadn't released a record since 1991, and the last time Shields performed in public, it was as a member of Primal Scream. Patti also had never publicly read *The Coral Sea*—the epic, elegiac prose poem she wrote in a fugue after the death of Robert Mapplethorpe—because it was too emotionally loaded for her to even consider it.

Patti invited Shields because she had loved the loud, energetic noise landscapes of My Bloody Valentine's 1991 album *Loveless*. She heard something in that record that made her believe Shields would instinctively understand what she wanted to do, and she wasn't wrong. They never rehearsed, having only spent a couple of hours one afternoon discussing her vision for the performance. Despite it being 100 percent improvised, that night's version of *The Coral Sea* is emotional and incandescent; Shields's improvisation is bright, delicate, and perfectly suited to the text, which describes Mapplethorpe's life through the metaphor of a lengthy sea voyage.

As a performance piece, it excels, but it does not

lend itself to repeated listening (the Meltdown outing was released on CD). I struggle with the text; there are some beautiful passages, but I find it challenging to see Mapplethorpe in it despite what Patti has said about its origin.

What interests me most about *The Coral Sea* is tracing the direct and fairly definitive line from the improvisational ethos in "Birdland" to "Radio Ethiopia" to "Spell" to this performance, which is connected by a dotted line through *peace and noise*'s "Memento Mori" and "Radio Baghdad" on *Trampin'*, arriving at the work Patti has recently done with Soundwalk Collective. All of this is built on her belief in the power of improvisation and her love of jazz, and relies on her innate skills as a performer and her ability to collaborate in live performance with rock and roll musicians. Patti isn't a band leader in the tradition established by the early Black pioneers like James Brown, Jackie Wilson, or Sam & Dave, all of whom you can see in the live concert presentations of Bruce Springsteen and Prince, but she can still move with and guide the direction of a performance through voice, breath, and energy.

Patti Smith's Meltdown curation was widely heralded by the media, the performers, and the attendees. Part of this praise was due to the fact that the explicitly experimental nature of the festival meant that audiences were both attentive and forgiving, and performances that may not have worked onstage were still saluted for their effort. But the other element was that for much of the UK and

Europe, Patti Smith's place as an artist and a cultural arbiter is unquestioned.

Immediately after Meltdown, Patti traveled to Paris to officially receive the title *Commandeur des Arts et des Lettres*. The award has three levels, with *commandeur* being the highest, and it recognizes eminent writers and artists who have contributed significantly to furthering the arts in France. The medal itself is a beautifully regal gilt-and-green enameled asterisk hanging from a green-and-white striped ribbon. Only twenty *commandeur* ribbons can be awarded per year, and previous American recipients include Paul Auster, Ornette Coleman, Jim Jarmusch, Meryl Streep, and Robert Redford.

Patti is particularly proud of this honor; it is always mentioned in her biographical material, and it is prominently displayed in her house (based on the many photographs we've seen of it arranged in various assemblages and altars). If I had won this prize, I would wear the medal everywhere, even to the grocery store and laundromat, so good for her.

Two years later, Patti finally got the call from the Rock & Roll Hall of Fame. She was first eligible for induction in 2001, twenty-six years after the release of *Horses*.[11] She was nominated every year thereafter but not inducted until 2007. It should not have taken that long. By comparison, the first wave of punk bands were allowed in the Rock Hall in 2002, starting with the Ramones and Talking Heads. The UK branch of the family made their entrance in 2003 with the Clash, Elvis Costello, and the Police. Blondie and the Sex Pistols followed in 2006. Patti had already attended the ceremony as a presenter, inducting Clive Davis in 2000, the Velvet Underground in 1996, and, of course, Lou Reed as a solo artist in 2015.

It escaped absolutely no one's notice that Patti's induction coincided with that of R.E.M. Sure, it could have been a complete coincidence that a band fronted by Michael Stipe, a longtime and outspoken fan, champion, and now friend of his teenage hero, was being inducted in their first year of eligibility at the exact same time that the Rock Hall nominating committee finally capitulated to induct Patti,[12] but it seems suspect. She should have been a first-ballot Hall of Famer, but she was in. Finally.

The Rock & Roll Hall of Fame is problematic on many levels. An entire book could be written about its omissions, late takes, and epic misogyny. But the Rock Hall matters because it matters. For many of the artists honored, it can be an essential validation in a career that may have not provided fame, popular recognition, or royalties. Induction is supposed to be an affirmation of excellence, talent, and impact, and when the Hall gets it right, there is magic and drama and all kinds of cosmic redemption. If you get the chance to attend a ceremony during a year that one of your bands is being inducted, the evening feels like a combination wedding reception and senior prom: people are dressed up, fans congratulate each other for their band's induction, and you will both clap so hard your hands hurt and cry your eyes out.

Patti would allude to all of this in "Ain't It Strange," the op-ed she wrote for the *New York Times* on the eve of her induction, noting that she struggled with the institutional recognition and her own place within it. She shared that Fred had believed one day she would receive the recognition she was due and asked that she accept it in his name: "Fred Sonic Smith was of the people, and I am none but him: one who has loved rock 'n' roll and crawled from the ranks to the stage."[13] He also asked her to promise not to swear.

And she would represent the ranks in the pages of the *Times* as well, sharing the communal warmth and recognition she had received from random strangers since the announcement: "And a shout from the sanitation man driving down my street: 'Hey, Patti. Hall of Fame. One for us.' I just smiled, and I noticed that I was proud. One for the neighborhood. My parents. My band. One for Fred. And anybody else who wants to come along."[14]

At the ceremony, Rage Against the Machine's Zack de la Rocha (a reasonable though not obvious choice) did the honors. His induction speech was warm, intelligent, and heartfelt. There was a camera on Patti waiting backstage, watching her reaction to the speech. Her expression is a mixture of terror and nervousness; after a few minutes, she turns away and faces the wall behind her (this would happen once or twice more before they gave up trying for live reaction shots).

De la Rocha's tribute balanced the breadth of her contributions and impact, giving equal time to punk rock, poetry, and politics. He said, "The movement she helped define explained why people like me related more to the Bad Brains than the Eagles, why we championed the Clash and hated Ronald Reagan, and why we dropped our textbooks and picked up Sonia Sanchez, Allen Ginsberg, and Langston Hughes, expanding rock's boundaries. Patti Smith the poet revealed truth, regardless of the political or social consequences."[15]

A visibly emotional Patti, dressed in *Horses* suit and tie, embraced de la Rocha for an extended interval before gripping the statue and approaching the podium. In tears, she assured the audience, "I'm very proud and happy to be here, and if it seems like I'm not, it's just that so many people that I love, that are so happy for me, have a different seat. They're a bit higher up."[16] She pointed skyward. Patti invoked her parents, her brother, and her husband, before extending gratitude to Clive Davis and Columbia Records and then her managers and advisers Jane Friedman, Ina Meibach, and Rosemary Carroll.

"Rock and roll is a collective, it's a brotherhood," she went on to say, paying tribute to Richard Sohl and Ivan Král, and then Oliver Ray and Tom Verlaine. This was followed by a special shout-out to the road crew, of course, including her late brother Todd: "We are nothing without our crews." She acknowledged Jesse and Jackson, noting that he would be performing with them, before arriving at "my present band": Tony Shanahan, Jay Dee (who was specifically recognized for the longevity of his tenure), and, finally, closing with "my good friend and collaborator, but mostly my good friend and champion, Lenny Kaye."[17]

The inductees usually perform three songs, and the PSG chose "Gimme Shelter," with Patti noting, "We'd like to thank Keith Richards for being amongst us."[18] Patti and the band performed "Because the Night" and then "RnRN," which was accompanied by an explanatory clip from Patti regarding the history of the song. It was a strong performance for the band, and certainly one worthy of the occasion. As the performance progressed, Patti looked less nervous and more comfortable.

But the real fun happened during R.E.M.'s set, when Patti and Lenny joined the boys from Athens, Georgia, for a cheery rendition of "I Wanna Be Your Dog," an R.E.M. favorite but also a not-so-silent protest at the Stooges still not being in the Hall. Patti and Michael were utterly adorable together, singing with and at each other; she kept grabbing him by the waist and pulling him in closer until he finally broke into a big grin. (As I watched, I kept thinking of the stories Stipe had told of his teenage self sitting in his bedroom and listening to Patti, and how that kid had no idea that thirty-some years later he would be singing a proto-punk classic that was near and dear to his heart with one of his heroes the night his band was inducted into the Rock & Roll Hall of Fame.)

"People Have the Power" was the closing jam session, which, in the pre-HBO years of the Rock Hall, was always an experiment in chaos and serendipity. The challenge was that not everyone on the stage knew the song. Things would have been fine if the main performers had been limited to Patti, Michael Stipe, and Eddie Vedder, but the mic got passed to both Ronnie Spector and Sammy Hagar, who were not, shall we say, quite as conversant with the material. Guitar solos went to Keith Richards and Steven Stills, with mixed results. Even with the disarray, it was a small serving of karmic justice to have one of Patti's songs be the closing number, and for it to be one of Fred Smith's songs (and no, the MC5 are *still* not in, as of 2021) just doubled it.

"The people have the power / to redeem the work of fools." It's corny, but yes, they did.

Despite a loud chorus of "Finally!" from a wide range of fans and admirers upon Patti's induction into the Rock & Roll Hall of Fame, there was a faction that was furious—not at the Hall of Fame, but at Patti's presumption that she belonged within this mostly male-dominated pantheon that commemorates the mostly male-dominated arena of rock and roll. She did not put herself forward, yet somehow she was at fault for having been chosen.

The primary voice of this faction belonged to Bob Lefsetz, a music industry analyst with a popular newsletter.

Mr. Lefsetz (while being sure to snidely refer to her as "*Ms.*
Smith," which is the only way a misogynist readily uses
that honorific) insisted at least half a dozen times that she
didn't belong because (among other things) he personally
does not listen to her records and because "the only people
who care are those who lived in Manhattan in the seventies."[19] He further asserted multiple times that her "only
hit" was written by Bruce Springsteen, despite the documented cowriting credit.

Do you know who else gets mentioned in the *Lefsetz
Letter* as a "fraudster"[20] undeserving of their places in the
Rock & Roll Hall of Fame? Joan Jett. Blondie. Whitney
Houston. Who does Mr. Lefsetz applaud? Ann and Nancy
Wilson, because "they were from Seattle, and they were
CUTE!"[21] According to him, they belong in the Hall of
Fame not because of their songwriting or musicianship,
but because they fit a narrow gender binary.

The classicist Mary Beard, in her book *Women and
Power*, notes that "right where written evidence for
Western culture starts, women's voices are not being heard
in the public sphere" and that "women, even when they are
not silenced, still have to pay a very high price for being
heard."[22] There is a well-known Roman epithet, *vir bonus
dicendi peritus* (a good man, skilled in speaking), which,
if taken to its logical conclusion, meant that "a woman
speaking in public was, in most circumstances, by definition not a woman."[23] All of this is to say that Mr. Lefsetz was not as original a thinker as he fancied himself;

moreover, he serves an infuriating reminder of how toxic masculinity still reigns within the music business.

While I appreciate all aspects of Patti Smith's career, my drug of choice is to see her in concert. I got to see her only once in the 1970s, and it was not that it exceeded my expectations — it was that I didn't know that what she did was something I could *expect*. My heart was broken when she moved to Michigan because I wanted to see her again, this time knowing what to expect and not being so overwhelmed by it that I walked back to the train feeling like a cartoon character who had been knocked on the head and had little birds circling above.

When she returned in the '90s, I never got tired of walking into Bowery Ballroom at the end of every year and being able to celebrate her birthday or ring in the New Year with her as the soundtrack. Her shows are never boring, they are never the same, they are always different, they always surprise me. I am amazed that she is still such a compelling performer. Even though I have attended hundreds of concerts by a wide variety of artists, I never pass up an opportunity to see her live (something I cannot say truthfully about a lot of other artists I love).

The construction and vibe of her current live performance is not dissimilar to what you would have seen back in the day. She reads poetry, she talks to the audience, and Lenny gets a solo spot where he offers "a Nugget if you dug it!" Patti gets a minute to rest her voice or dance next to the drum riser. There are plenty of Johnny Carson–esque one-liners. When her children are part of the band, a whole other element is introduced. It's a reminder of what this phase of her work could have been if her husband were still alive, and it also introduces some hilarity when she tells a story or says something to one of the kids and they roll their eyes at each other in a way that only siblings can. It is a different energy and a different intensity; while it is more measured and controlled, it can still be overwhelming. I have screamed and cried and prayed and danced at her shows, sometimes all on the same night.

It doesn't feel disingenuous when Patti performs "Land" at age seventy. The way she can completely flip the energy in the venue just by saying the words "The boy was in the hallway / drinking a glass of tea" is a stunning example of her abilities. That declaration silences conversations; it draws people to sharp attention. In performance, "Land" is a shamanic experience like no other. But you can say that about a lot of Patti's work: "Birdland" is on that list for sure, as is "Ain't It Strange," "Free Money," and "Beneath the Southern Cross." These songs walk a tightrope between poetry and mysticism. You always go with her and you want to see where she ends up. It feels genuine, authentic, not an act, not a gimmick. Not that gimmicks are bad; some gimmicks act as rituals and the power of ritual is in their repetition, such as Patti removing her boots during the bridge of "Dancing Barefoot" in the early run of shows in 1995. She creates connection, empathy, and shared sacred space.

The reason "Land" still works as a rock song and as a performance over forty years later is because it emanates from the place Patti started — *three-chord rock merged with the power of the word* — that connection to the ground floor basics of good rock and roll. That ethos feels like the essence that is grounding Patti and the band every night onstage and how it can, at worst, give you a great night of rock music, and at best, have you walk out feeling in your bones that you have profoundly experienced *something else*.

The other reason the older material still resonates is that Patti Smith as a musician never stopped moving. She did not want to be a nostalgia act; she did not want to be touring against her first four records for the rest of her life. The same creative energy required to write and record new music also fuels the internal combustion engine of the band in live performance. It is different, for certain, than it was forty years ago: the musicians are more proficient at their instruments and better at aligning their energy to last an entire show. But it is still as affirming and exciting as it ever was.

"She was a real rock and roll shaman, you know," Bruce Springsteen said, when asked about Patti as a live performer, "and the real ones come few and far between and she was one of those and she keeps getting better at her writing, and she's always a source of inspiration. So, it's lovely that she's sort of taken on this mantle of magic."[24]

"Magic" is an accurate description of her memorable performance at Glastonbury in 2015. Patti had played the storied British music festival previously, but this was the first time she was appearing on the Pyramid Stage, the festival's main stage. To no one's amazement, she made every single moment count, including abdicating a part of her set to bring out none other than the Dalai Lama. The footage was an amazing thing to watch, one of the originators of punk rock bringing out this man of peace, who also happened to be someone Patti personally admired. It was deeply moving to see Patti, the schoolgirl who wrote a book report about the Tibetan people in the late '50s, share her space with him and treasure the moment.

During the performance, you could hear that Patti's voice was rough after touring for the previous six weeks, but it didn't affect her energy. The eternal British summer rain, however, did have an impact as it caused her to slip and fall onto the stage during the last song of the set, her cover of the Who's "My Generation." The song's been in the setlist forever, but it was especially interesting that night considering that the actual Who were the festival headliners. So, she was performing the song standing next to Pete Townshend's amp, which might or might not have had anything to do with what happened next: she sang the song with as much conviction as ever, ripped the strings off her guitar, and declared, "Yeah, I fell on my fucking ass at Glastonbury. That's because I'm a fucking animal!" The *Telegraph* declared, "Patti Smith may have just delivered the set of the weekend."[25]

A hallmark of Patti's live concerts is the way she almost always grounds the show in the city or the venue. When she's at the Fillmore in San Francisco, she'll evoke Hendrix or Joplin or Garcia, someone with a connection to the community. She will remember birthdays and death days by reading a poem or telling a story.

In 2001, the band came to Seattle, where I was living at the time, as part of the opening weekend for the Experience Music Project,[26] the billionaire Paul Allen's excuse to own a bunch of Jimi Hendrix memorabilia. Of course, they opened the show with "Hey Joe." The concert was held at the Mural Amphitheater, an outdoor stage below the Space Needle that was built as part of Seattle Center, the complex built in 1962 for the World's Fair. The amphitheater has been the location of many amazing and important shows in Seattle, but Seattle Center will also be remembered by music fans of a certain age as the location where a candlelight vigil was held two days after Kurt Cobain's suicide. I'm pretty sure Patti didn't know any of that, but she knew she was in Seattle, and probably in the back of my mind I thought we would get "About a Boy" in the setlist. I didn't think I would witness a high and lonesome version of Nirvana's "Heart-Shaped Box" featuring Patti and Oliver at the front of the stage, with Oliver strumming his guitar as hard as he could, keening at the end, and Patti picking up her Tibetan singing bowl to add to the energy and soothe the loss.

A lot of people come to Seattle and do Kurt Cobain tributes, and they are often ill-fitting and insincere. Not this one.[27]

In 2016, Patti Smith was invited to perform at the 2016 Nobel Prize ceremony to honor the laureate for literature. She is revered in Sweden and had won the nation's Polar Music Prize a few years earlier. The invitation arrived before the winner had been made public, so she picked one of her own songs—she has never said which one—and looked forward to a few days in Stockholm.

And then Bob Dylan was announced as the winner of the 2016 Nobel Prize in Literature.

I guess it's not entirely surprising that Dylan wouldn't just issue a press release thanking the Swedish Academy and then show up at the ceremony to accept his award like most mere mortals. Instead, he didn't even acknowledge the award for almost two weeks after the announcement, explaining that he was "speechless," which is hilarious given that he had just won the Nobel Prize for Literature. When he finally did respond, it was only to decline to attend the ceremony, citing "pre-existing commitments." The entire world was glued to this saga because the Swedish Academy was blogging about it and complaining to the media. So what should have been a cut-and-dried situation became the subject of breathless updates on CNN and NPR.

In the middle of this was Patricia Lee Smith, who was now representing Bob Dylan at the ceremony and what was supposed to be an enjoyable trip was now an international incident. She no longer felt it was appropriate to sing one of her songs and questioned whether she should even perform at all, fretting, "Would this displease Bob Dylan, whom I would never desire to displease?"[28] She decided that she should instead sing one of his songs, "A Hard Rain's A-Gonna Fall."

She knew the song; she had sung it onstage before, twice with her late husband. Still, Patti being Patti, that wasn't sufficient. In a piece she wrote about the experience for the *New Yorker*, she said, "From that moment, every spare moment was spent practicing it, making certain that I knew and could convey every line."[29]

Watching the video of the ceremony is enough to give you a case of the jitters. Everything in the Stockholm Concert Hall is perfect and precise; the audience members are dressed in finery surpassing any ceremony short of a royal wedding; the hall is filled with many of the brilliant minds of our time. Chosen to represent Bob Dylan is a lone woman from New Jersey, singing one of his more complex compositions (the only harder choices would have been either "Desolation Row" or "It's Alright, Ma [I'm Only Bleeding]," the former for its verbosity, the latter for the specificity of its cadence). She does not have the safety and comfort of her band, but is instead standing in front of a full orchestra, even if only a few of them are accompanying her.

She begins the song without incident, getting through the first verse and charging into the second. But after the first few lines, she begins to sound hesitant, and she's mixing lyrics from different lines, before apologizing multiple times and then asking if they could start that section again. "I apologize. Sorry, I'm so nervous." The crowd applauds, and Patti finishes the song.

It wasn't that she had forgotten the words. As she wrote in the *New Yorker*, "I was struck with a plethora of emotions, avalanching with such intensity that I was unable to negotiate them."[30] The musicians, with exceeding professionalism, continue the melody so that she can resume the verse. Except she is unable to. Instead, she pauses, begs forgiveness, and asks if they can start the verse again. The audience applauds in warmth and solidarity, and Patti finishes the rest of the song without much further issue, even though she is privately mortified at what she viewed as a failure.

But the next morning at breakfast, she was greeted by many of the Nobel scientists, who told her, "For us, your performance seemed a metaphor for our own struggles." It seems unfortunate that she did not see that she responded to the moment in the same way she always has responded: she accepted the job even if she wasn't 100 percent certain, she did her best, she did not try to hide her mistake, she apologized for it, she tried again, and she succeeded. In 2018, she spoke with an interviewer about what it was like to perform with her children, and she said, "I always told them, 'Don't worry if you mess up or if I mess up—just do the best you can and stay in communication.' "[31]

This is fantastic advice in almost every occupation, and it has served Patti well in everything she has ever accomplished, from writing a play with Sam Shepard to playing guitar or clarinet onstage to this tribute to Dylan. I saw her at the Tibet House benefit at Carnegie Hall a few months after the ceremony and was thrilled that "Hard Rain" was part of her set. Its inclusion was a typical response for Patti: she knew everyone had heard about what happened, and instead of just ignoring that fact, she stood there on that stage and sang it again for all of us. Her performance was spellbinding, the intensity building as she worked her way through it, and she got a standing ovation at the song's end. The performance was worthy of that reaction, but it was also the audience telling her that we were on her side. Because we were.

CBGB, the club where Patti started and punk blossomed, lost its lease in the early '00s, and after a prolonged battle, the club announced it was shutting its doors for good on Sunday, October 15, 2006. Patti Smith and her band were chosen to close the place down for the last time, following a whirlwind of last-chance appearances by CB's veterans like Bad Brains, the Dictators, and Blondie. The night of the last show, it was absolute chaos outside, with news trucks, tourists wandering by, fans without tickets trying to get in, and a series of street musicians improvising songs about CBGB.

Inside was also chaotic: it was hot, the sound was poor, the show was being broadcast over the radio, and there were multiple technical issues. (To be fair, except for the radio broadcast, that could describe pretty much any show at CB's.) The band had to stop and start the Marvelettes' "The Hunter Gets Captured by the Game" three times before getting it right. The same thing happened with the Velvet Underground's "Pale Blue Eyes." We didn't care. It was the last night, and she could have played until the sun came up and no one would have left.

Patti yelled at Richard Lloyd of Television to stop worrying about tuning his guitar, and then they covered "Marquee Moon" before playing "We Three," a song about the very floor on which we were standing. Flea from the Red Hot Chili Peppers showed up to play bass on "My Generation." They covered the Ramones and the Dead Boys and the Rolling Stones. I cried during "Land." Patti cried during "Land." And at the end, she sang "Elegie" and read a long list of names, everyone from our tribe that we had lost to drugs or disease or simply the annals of time and old age.

She was the right person to end this era of music history not just because she was the first one to break out and the first one to draw wider attention to the music that was emanating from this dark, narrow, neon-lit club. She deserved the honor because she could see both the big picture and the intimate details of history and respond to that context. She didn't just get up onstage and play a show (although she did because that is what she always did at CBGB); she got up there and reminded us of why it was important, of what happened in that place, of everyone who made it what it was, and why we should never forget it.

In early spring 2020, Patti and the band headed out west to perform some warmup shows in Los Angeles, San Francisco, and Seattle before heading to Australia and New Zealand. In 2017, Patti had matter-of-factly stated that her shows Down Under would likely be the last time she performed in those countries, as she didn't expect that her health would permit her to return. It was therefore wonderful news to those fans—and, in effect, all her fans—that she felt she was strong enough to embark on such a tour again. In fact, 2020 was intended to be a year of expansive touring all over the globe. For this to happen in what would be her seventy-fourth year was remarkable.

The first two shows were at San Francisco's fabled Fillmore, home of many a legendary Patti Smith show and sparkling with the fairy dust of years of rock and roll history. Since there had been no birthday / New Year's shows in 2019, I made my way to San Francisco for the performances.

It was early March, still a week away from the COVID-19 pandemic dominating our lives in the United States. At the time of the shows, the biggest thing I worried about was not touching the stage and, when I inevitably forgot, to not touch my face until I could wash my hands. Patti joked about it onstage, rubbing elbows with Tony Shanahan. In our defense, we did not know. I was planning on doing some research while in town at various archives and libraries, only to have those plans thwarted as the state and the city began to take steps to protect Californians against the virus. I made it out of San Francisco the day before the total lockdown.

Those would be the last two concerts I would see in 2020 and well into 2021. The band made it to Seattle only to have the concert there canceled shortly thereafter. Tour dates in the future were postponed and then canceled or rescheduled. In the middle of quarantine, I reflected that if Patti Smith and her Band at the Fillmore was the last rock show I got to see, at least I went out on a high note.

EPILOGUE: GRATEFUL

In 1980, I remember reading a small item in a music magazine something that confirmed my worst fears: the lack of any Patti Smith sightings in any of the usual places meant that she was gone. She departed just as I arrived, and once again I bemoaned being born too late for anything cool.

In a million years, I never thought I would be standing in front of a stage fifteen years later waiting for her to walk onto it and that, after that, this would become a normal part of my life in the ensuing decades. That I would have a chance to sing the old songs and a chance to learn new ones. That there would be new art and new writing. That every December, I could walk into the Bowery Ballroom and wish her happy birthday or throw confetti to celebrate the New Year. That she would, through some miracle of the universe, continue to be a thrilling, inspiring live performer.

I did not think I would get to grow old with her, to watch as she fought her gray hair and then finally gave up, and through that action, be given the courage to do the same. I did not know how meaningful it would be to exist within the current of her art, to have the continuity of her entire body of work easily available and published under her aegis, to be able to pursue it and study it and examine it, and not to emulate her but to be consistently motivated and inspired by her art and her example.

Patti Smith taught us how to kick the doors in, and she continues to teach us how to live with integrity, to keep our name clean, to take chances, to keep the memories of our loved ones alive, to continue after they're gone, even when we think we cannot, and how to persevere through it all.

And most importantly, she taught us to do the work, and to just keep doing the work.

ACKNOWLEDGMENTS

I have a habit of saying I am going to do things, and then when I do them, I am astonished that the thing has happened. That is absolutely the case right now. It seems impossible that I have written a book about Patti Smith, yet here it is. I will never stop being thrilled that Patti Smith is still making music, performing, and shaking out the ghost dance, and I thank her for all of it.

Thanks to the New York Public Library for granting me access to their Research Study Rooms for six months. Having a quiet place to work that was also close to the research materials I needed was invaluable, and every single person at the library with whom I interacted was unfailingly helpful. Librarians rule and the NYPL is the absolute best.

Thanks to the Fales Library at New York University for access to their vast archive of punk rock and downtown documents and ephemera.

No one wants to go on the record saying anything about Patti Smith even if it's positive, so my profound thanks to the people who did: Theresa Kereakes, Jay Dee Daugherty, and Bruce Springsteen.

Marilyn Laverty at Shore Fire Media was instrumental in helping me obtain a vital piece of research, and I thank her for both her professionalism and enthusiasm.

My editor, Casey Kittrell, warmly welcomed me to the University of Texas Press family and extended endless patience and encouragement.

Evelyn McDonnell pulled me into the *Women Who Rock* project and then asked me if there was anyone I wanted to write about for a new series she was editing. Thank you for your faith and tireless quest for excellence. I am thrilled to be part of the Music Matters family.

Evie Nagy and Holly George-Warren provided peer reviews of the manuscript. I could not have asked for better reviewers. Their thoughtful analysis and suggestions improved this book, and I am grateful for their feedback.

Dr. Charles Hughes truly epitomizes a "you gotta walk it, talk it, in your heart" ethos. I am so glad we met all those years ago at the first Springsteen symposium.

Dave Marsh's early writing on Patti had a tremendous impact on both my understanding of her work and the kind of writer I would become, and I am grateful for his work and his mentorship.

I would not have gotten through writing this book without the group chat: Alison Fensterstock, Hilary Hughes, Maura Johnston, Marissa M. Moss, and Annie Zaleski. Thank you all for being a sounding board, a cheering squad, and unstoppable hype women. They all have books coming out, please go and buy them. Hire them to write things for you.

Jamison Foser agreed to be an early reader and offered thoughtful, smart, informed feedback. I am so glad we are friends.

Chris Phillips and *Backstreets Magazine* have always given me space to report on the Springsteen/Smith connections and offered advice and encouragement, and I'm grateful to have written for them for almost two decades.

Emma Span, Jay Jaffe, and Robin Span-Jaffe were singlehandedly responsible for getting me out of the house, feeding me, and keeping me afloat when the chips were down.

Heather Campbell, Shirley Carlson, Mairead Case, Jen Cubias, Jessica Hopper, Holly Gleason, Muffy Kroha, Elisa Leon, Jessica Letkemann, Melody Malosh, Karyn Brown Meszaros, Lisa Messier, Ann Powers, Jill Sternheimer, Teresa Soito and Greg Breit, Matt Wardlaw, Susan Whitall, and others extended their friendship and moral support generally and also helped buoy me through a particularly challenging time to be writing.

To the many Patti Smith friends and fans I've met across the decades who didn't want to be quoted, thank you for your friendship and sisterhood.

And finally, thanks to my dear friend, the late Holly Cara Price, for always showing a little faith. I am so sorry you aren't here to see this, but I know you're watching.

In addition to the sources cited in the notes, I would also like to acknowledge the following:

The Patti Smith Setlists website, available at http://setlists .pattismithlogbook.info/.

Anthony Rzepela and Fiona Webster, whose collections of Patti articles online — many of which were typed by hand back in ye olden days of the internet — helped me kickstart this project.

The tapers of the world: my heartfelt gratitude to anyone who ever taped a show, encoded it, restored it, or put it online. You are truly unsung heroes.

NOTES

Preface

1. Unofficial audience recording of Patti Smith's "One Book, One New York" presentation at Symphony Space, May 10, 2019.
2. Jacob Uitti, "Patti Smith Is Always Going to Be a Worker," *Interview*, October 2, 2020, www.interviewmagazine.com/music/patti-smith-is -always-going-to-be-a-worker.

1. Three Chords Merged with the Power of the Word

1. From the "officially" released recording of the performance, *February 10, 1971* (Mer Records, 2006).
2. Patti Smith, *Just Kids* (New York: HarperCollins, 2010), 138.
3. Ibid., 182.
4. A bootleg for years, Polk's recording was officially released on Patti and Lenny's own Mer Records, and you can legally buy it today via your favorite music retailer. Brigid Polk is also remembered for her 1970 recording of the Velvet Underground's *Live at Max's Kansas City* album, on which none other than Jim Carroll can be heard repeatedly asking the server to get him a Pernod from the downstairs bar.
5. Smith, *Just Kids*, 184.
6. Anna Elizabeth Balakian, *The Symbolist Movement: Critical Appraisal* (New York: Random House, 1968), 4.
7. Later I realized that a woman would never have been allowed to get that far at that time and that reaching that point almost killed Dylan.
8. Smith, *Just Kids*, 181.
9. Joan Juliet Buck, "The Private World of Patti Smith," *Harper's Bazaar*, October 30, 2015, www.harpersbazaar.com/culture/features/a12479 /patti-smith-1115/.
10. Ibid.

11. Ibid.
12. Smith, *Just Kids*, 25.
13. Ibid., 17.
14. Ibid., 31.
15. It may be gorgeous again someday, but it has been scaffolded and under renovation for almost a decade, as part of its inevitable conversion into a boutique hotel.
16. Smith, *Just Kids*, 183.
17. Lisa Robinson, "Patti Smith: The High Priestess of Rock and Roll," *Hit Parader*, January 1976.
18. Smith, *Just Kids*, 182–183.
19. Ibid., 218.
20. Patti Smith, "Dog Dream," in *Collected Lyrics, 1970–2015* (New York: HarperCollins, 2015), 11.
21. As quoted by Ben Edmonds in "Heaven's Hired Hand: Reconnecting with Patti Smith," *Addicted to Noise*, July 1995.
22. Smith, *Just Kids*, 232.
23. Ibid., 238.
24. He does — it's uncanny.
25. The Academy of Music was later known as the Palladium.
26. Kembrew McLeod, *The Downtown Pop Underground* (New York: Abrams, 2018), 361.
27. Ibid., 381.
28. Ibid., 362.
29. Clinton Heylin, *From the Velvets to the Voidoids: A Pre-Punk History for a Post-Punk World* (London: Penguin, 1993), 133.
30. Devorah Ostrov, "Kaye Tells: From Nuggets to Doc Rock to the Patti Smith Group," https://reetmag.wixsite.com/reetmag/lennykaye.
31. A "cut-out" is a piece of physical media, such as a record album, whose cover has been marked in some way (a corner cut off, a hole punched, or a notch cut) to denote that a store had returned it as unsold. The manufacturers would resell the records at a discounted price, and stores then placed them in bargain or cut-out bins. Promo records usually got the same treatment so they couldn't be sold as new.
32. Smith, *Just Kids*, 241.

33. Smith, "Piss Factory," in *Collected Lyrics*, 27.
34. Interview with the author, January 2021.
35. Interview with the author, December 2020.
36. Ostrov, "Kaye Tells."
37. Smith, *Just Kids*, 244.
38. *Dancing Barefoot*, directed by Zdenek Suchý (Prague: Česká televize, 1995).
39. *Rock Scene*, September 1976.
40. Heylin, *From the Velvets*, 133.
41. A noncommercial radio station in New York City, WBAI was a major countercultural organ.
42. Email with the author, June 2021.
43. Ibid.
44. James Wolcott, "When Bob Dylan Called on Patti Smith," *Village Voice*, July 7, 1975.
45. Ibid.
46. Smith, *Just Kids*, 248.
47. Patti Smith, "We Can Be Heroes," *Details*, July 1993.
48. Susan Shapiro, "Patti Smith: Somewhere, Over the Rimbaud," *Crawdaddy*, December 1975.
49. Dave Marsh, "Her Horses Got Wings, They Can Fly," *Rolling Stone*, January 1, 1976.
50. Ed Vulliamy, " 'Some give a song. Some give a life... ,' " *Guardian*, June 3, 2005.
51. I regret to inform you that the music business is still sexist and retrograde.
52. At a Van Morrison tribute show at Carnegie Hall in 2019, Patti noted that Van always hated her version.
53. The 1988 *Dream of Life* is the one record that doesn't include any kind of improvisational number.
54. Smith, *Just Kids*, 249.
55. Tony Hiss and David McClelland, "Gonna Be So Big, Gonna Be a Star, Watch Me Now!," *New York Times Magazine*, December 21, 1975.
56. Lisa Robinson, *There Goes Gravity: A Life in Rock and Roll* (New York: Riverhead Books, 2014), 6.
57. Marsh, "Her Horses Got Wings."

2. C'mon, God, Make a Move

1. Benmont Tench, the keyboard player for Tom Petty and the Heartbreakers, commented to me that this was a frequent problem with keyboard players on *SNL*.
2. I don't know whether this was a thing anywhere else, but people did this in both my middle school and my high school.
3. Amy Gross, "Introducing Rock 'N' Roll's Lady Raunch: Patti Smith," *Mademoiselle*, September 1975.
4. Ibid.
5. Chris Brazier, "The Resurrection of Patti Smith," *Melody Maker*, March 18, 1978.
6. Charles Shaar Murray, "Patti Smith: *Radio Ethiopia*," *New Musical Express*, October 23, 1976.
7. Robert Christgau, "Patti Smith: Save This Rock and Roll Hero," *Village Voice*, January 17, 1977.
8. Fred Schruers, "Patti Smith Riding Crest of New Wave," *Circus*, May 1978.
9. MaryKate Clearly, " 'But Is It Art?': Constantin Brancusi vs. the United States," *Inside/Out*, July 24, 2014, www.moma.org/explore/inside _out/2014/07/24/but-is-it-art-constantin-brancusi-vs-the-united-states/.
10. There are exceptions to this, of course, where the headliners specifically invite bands they like or have been influenced by or think are interesting as a way of curating the evening for fans.
11. John Rockwell, "The Pop Life," *New York Times*, April 15, 1977.
12. Hilary Hughes, "Patti Smith on 'Because the Night' at 40: How Her Bruce Springsteen Collaboration Is 'A Whole Life in a Song,' " *Billboard*, June 21, 2018.
13. The title of the song is explicit on the album and in all of Patti's books. That is her choice to make. In addition to the name of the song being abbreviated as "RnRN," the word will be redacted throughout. I understand that I am doing this in cases where the writer deliberately chose to use the word, but this book has my name on it, and I do not use that word. Full stop.
14. *The Defiant Ones*, episode 1, directed by Allen Hughes, aired July 9, 2017, on HBO.
15. Hughes, "Patti Smith."

16. Some stories have Iovine driving Springsteen down to Coney Island; in others, they're sitting in a hotel lobby. The venue is different, but the conversation is always the same.

17. Interview with the author, January 2021.

18. *The Defiant Ones*, episode 1.

19. It also went gold in Italy, which certifies more than twenty-five thousand units, as per Federazione Industria Musicale Italiana.

20. Interview with the author, January 2021.

21. John Tobler, "15 Minutes with Patti Smith," *ZigZag*, October 1978.

22. Interview with the author, January 2021. Springsteen would have to wait until the release of "Hungry Heart" in 1980 before he would have a song chart on the Hot 100.

23. *The Defiant Ones*, episode 1.

24. Hughes, "Patti Smith."

25. Charles M. Young, "Visions of Patti Smith," *Rolling Stone*, July 27, 1978.

26. You can easily find evidence of this on YouTube or any number of bootlegs.

27. Caryn Rose, "Patti Smith Group: *Easter*," *Pitchfork*, May 28, 2017, https://pitchfork.com/reviews/albums/23244-easter/.

28. Robert Christgau, "Patti Smith."

29. Nick Tosches, "Patti Smith Group: *Easter*," *CREEM*, June 1978.

30. Dave Marsh, "*Easter*," *Rolling Stone*, April 20, 1978.

31. Dael Orlandersmith, "Not a Rock N Roll N——r," in *Here She Comes Now: Women in Music Who Have Changed Our Lives*, edited by Jeff Gordinier and Marc Weingarten (Los Angeles: Rare Bird Books, 2015), 136, 137.

32. Tim Jonze, " 'You decide your fate. Are you going to fall apart or own it?,' " *Guardian*, June 16, 2016.

33. In the interest of fairness, I would like to note that "RnRN" has not been in the setlist in 2021.

34. But let's give Clive credit that he didn't push for it to be airbrushed out. When he gave Patti complete creative control, he meant it.

35. Hughes, "Patti Smith."

36. In Detroit, a coney island is a diner.

37. Patti Smith, *M Train* (New York: Knopf, 2015), 10.

38. Paul Myers, *A Wizard, a True Star: Todd Rundgren in the Studio* (London: Jawbone, 2010), chap. 14, Kindle ed.

39. Patti Smith Group, *Wave*, Arista AB 4221, 1979, 33⅓ rpm, liner notes.

40. Myers, *Wizard*, chap. 14.
41. Patti's math was close: Little Richard played the Park almost eleven years before on August 17, 1968.
42. Michael Anthony, "Concert Proves Patti Smith Can Be Bad," *Minneapolis Star Tribune*, June 29, 1979.
43. Michael Goldberg, "Patti Smith: The Boarding House, San Francisco," *New Musical Express*, August 18, 1979.
44. Joan Juliet Buck, "The Private World of Patti Smith," *Harper's Bazaar*, October 30, 2015.
45. Associated Press, September 11, 1979.
46. Lisa Robinson, "Back from the Edge," *Elle*, May 1996.
47. Ibid.

3. Just Bumming Around

1. Bob Reitman, "Bob Reitman vs Patti Smith," *The Bugle*, May 1978.
2. The church was founded in 1842 with a specific charter to serve the maritime community working on the Great Lakes and is perhaps best known for its rector ringing the church bell twenty-nine times — once for each life lost — when he heard the news about the SS *Edmund Fitzgerald* sinking.
3. Lisa Robinson, "Rock Talk," *Hit Parader*, April 1980. Robinson was known for making these types of fashion observations in her "Eleganza" column in *CREEM*.
4. Andy Schwartz, "Patti Smith," *New York Rocker*, April 1981.
5. This may indeed be true about the Smith family home both because of its age and because of the presence of a secret bookcase that offers access to the basement.
6. Lisa Robinson, *Nobody Ever Asked Me about the Girls: Women, Music, and Fame* (New York: Henry Holt, 2020), 92.
7. Patti Smith, *M Train* (New York: Knopf, 2015), 85, 87.
8. Patti Smith notebooks and manuscripts, Manuscripts and Archives Division, New York Public Library.
9. Alan Light, "Patti Smith's Eternal Flame," *Cuepoint*, February 12, 2015, https://medium.com/cuepoint/patti-smiths-eternal-flame-fcadf12a8417.
10. Patti Smith, *Just Kids* (New York: HarperCollins, 2010), 265.

11. Mary Anne Cassata, "Patti Smith: A Rock Visionary's New Dream," *Music Paper*, October 1988.

12. Patti Smith, *Complete, 1975–2006: Lyrics, Reflections and Notes for the Future* (New York: Doubleday, 1998), 134.

13. Fred Mills, "Smith on Smith," *Detroit Metro Times*, December 1, 2004. When Patti went on the road in '95, Jackson would often escape the venue to go listen to Green Day on his CD player rather than stand in the room while that song was performed.

14. Robert Christgau, "Christgau's Consumer Guide," *Village Voice*, August 30, 1988.

15. Quotation derived from an audience recording of performance.

16. Interview with the author, January 2021.

17. Chris Nelson, "The Punk Poet Speaks," *Addicted to Noise*, December 1997.

18. Lisa Robinson, "The Positive Sides of Your Power," *Interview*, May 1988.

19. Peter Howell, "Patti Smith Breaks Her Silence," *Addicted to Noise*, June 30, 1995.

20. Lisa Robinson, *There Goes Gravity: A Life in Rock and Roll* (New York: Riverhead Books, 2014), 314.

21. Patti Smith, *Woolgathering* (New York: New Directions, 2011), ix.

22. *Michigan Daily*, March 18, 1991, https://digital.bentley.umich.edu/midaily/mdp.39015094723734/523.

23. I was not living in the United States at the time, so I only heard about it much later.

24. Gary Graff, "Patti Smith Takes Nectarine Stage for Old Time's Sake," *Detroit Free Press*, n.d.

25. All quotations from this performance are derived from an unofficial audience recording.

26. Susan Whitall, "Patti Smith's Return Juices Up the Nectarine's Last Drop," *Detroit News*, April 8, 1991.

27. Ibid.

28. Robinson, "Positive Sides of Your Power."

29. Ben Edmonds, "The Rebel: Patti Smith," *Mojo*, August 1996.

30. Evelyn McDonnell, "Because the Night," *Village Voice*, August 1, 1995.

31. All quotations from this performance are derived from an unofficial audience recording.

32. AIDS is a syndrome and not a virus. I am quoting Patti as she spoke that day; it was 1993, and the general public's understanding of HIV and AIDS was not what it is now.

33. Sharon DeLano, "The Torch Singer," *New Yorker*, March 11, 2002.

34. Tony Clayton-Lea, "Smith X Southwest," *Irish Times*, June 3, 2011.

35. Neil Strauss, "Poet, Singer, Mother: Patti Smith Is Back," *New York Times*, December 12, 1995.

36. In a poignant coincidence, Rosemary was Jim Carroll's first wife.

37. DeLano, "Torch Singer."

38. From an unofficial audience recording of a speech Patti gave at Ginsberg's memorial service at the Cathedral Church of St. John the Divine.

39. Ben Edmonds, "Heaven's Hired Hand: Reconnecting with Patti Smith," *Addicted to Noise*, July 1995.

40. "Patti Smith," Allen Ginsberg Project, December 30, 2018, https://allenginsberg.org/2018/12/s-30-patti-smith/.

41. Edmonds, "Heaven's Hired Hand."

42. Ibid.

43. Ibid.

44. Michael Goldberg and Jaan Uhelszki, "The ATN Q&A: Patti Smith," *Addicted to Noise*, June 1996.

45. Victor Bockris and Roberta Bayley, *Patti Smith: An Unauthorized Biography* (New York: Simon and Schuster, 1999), 262.

46. McDonnell, "Because the Night."

4. She Walked Home

1. Various artists, "People Have the Power: Patti Smith's Live Return with Carolyn Striho and the Detroit Energy Asylum, the Phoenix, Toronto, Ontario, Canada, Wednesday July 5, 1995," MyLifeinConcert.com, January 7, 2012, https://mylifeinconcert.com/1970s/084-people-have-the-power-patti-smith-july-5-1995/.

2. Quotations from this performance are derived from an unofficial audience recording.

3. Holly George-Warren, "She Is Risen," *Option*, May 1996.

4. Patricia Morrisroe, *Mapplethorpe* (New York: Random House, 2016), 222.

5. Lisa Robinson, *Nobody Ever Asked Me about the Girls: Women, Music, and Fame* (New York: Henry Holt, 2020), 92.

6. Allison Stewart, "Alternative nation's last stand: Lollapalooza 1995, an oral history," *Washington Post*, August 11, 2015, www.washingtonpost .com/lifestyle/style/alternative-nations-last-stand-lollapalooza-1995 -an-oral-history/2015/08/10/cb6857e4-3087-11e5-8f36-18d1d501920d _story.html.

7. Al Giordano, "On the Road Again with Patti Smith and Bob Dylan," *Boston Phoenix*, January 1996, https://bostonphoenix.com/alt1/archive /music/reviews/01-04-96/DYLAN_SMITH_1.html.

8. Ben Edmonds, "The Rebel: Patti Smith," *Mojo*, August 1996.

9. Ibid.

10. Alastair McKay, "Dark Eyes and a Sardonic Smile: Patti Smith on Working with Bob Dylan," *Alternatives to Valium* (blog), March 3, 2009, https://alternativestovalium.blogspot.com/2009/03/dark-eyes-and -sardonic-smile-patti_03.html.

11. Ibid.

12. Ibid.

13. Ibid.

14. Edmonds, "The Rebel."

15. Ibid.

16. Patti actually met Jimi Hendrix the night the studio opened. Jane Friedman was handling the publicity and gave Patti an invitation. She tells this story in *Just Kids*.

17. Patti Smith, *Just Kids* (New York: HarperCollins, 2010).

18. Edmonds, "The Rebel."

19. Michael Goldberg and Jaan Uhelszki, "Lenny Kaye: Life Is to Be Lived," *Addicted to Noise*, June 1996.

20. Michael Goldberg and Jaan Uhelszki, "The ATN Q&A: Patti Smith," *Addicted to Noise*, June 1996.

21. Ibid.

22. Goldberg and Uhelszki, "Lenny Kaye."

23. James Wolcott, "The Bollocks," *New Yorker*, July 22, 1996.

24. James Wolcott, *Critical Mass: Four Decades of Essays, Reviews, Hand Grenades, and Hurrahs* (New York: Doubleday, 2013), 158.

25. Vivien Goldman, *Revenge of the She-Punks: A Feminist Music History from Poly Styrene to Pussy Riot* (Austin: University of Texas Press, 2019), 191.

26. Glenn Dixon, "Black Yodel No. 6," *Washington City Paper*, October 11, 1996.

27. Goldberg and Uhelszki, "ATN Q&A."

28. Peter Howell, "Patti Smith Breaks Her Silence," *Addicted to Noise*, June 30, 1995.

29. Fred Mills, "Smith on Smith," *Detroit Metro Times*, December 1, 2004.

30. Brian Smith, "Daughter of the Revolution," *Detroit Metro Times*, February 22, 2012.

31. *Patti Smith: Dream of Life*, directed by Steven Sebring (Palm Pictures, 2008).

32. Lawrence French and Frank Andrick, "Interview with Lenny Kaye, March '96," A Patti Smith Babelogue, www.oceanstar.com/patti/bio/lennyint.htm.

33. Marc Maron, "Patti Smith," October 19, 2020, in *WTF*, podcast, www.wtfpod .com/podcast/episode-1167-patti-smith.

34. Goldberg and Uhelszki, "Lenny Kaye."

35. Patti Smith, *de l'ame pour l'ame* (newsletter), issue 1, May 1976.

36. Sharon DeLano, "The Torch Singer," *New Yorker*, March 11, 2002.

37. NPR put this list together as part of its Turning the Tables project, dedicated to revising the popular music canon to focus on women. (Note: I am a contributor to TTT).

38. British chart data are drawn from the British Phonographic Society website, www.bpi.co.uk/. US chart data are drawn from the Recording Industry Association of America website, www.riaa.com/. The 1991 Levi's advertisement used "Should I Stay or Should I Go" from the 1982 *Combat Rock*.

39. DeLano, "Torch Singer."

40. Lynda Richardson, "Public Lives: Godmother of Punk Rock Is No Comeback Kid," *New York Times*, June 19, 2001.

41. Chris Nelson, "The Punk Poet Speaks," *Addicted to Noise*, December 1997.

42. Margit Detwiler, "20 Questions for Patti Smith," *Philadelphia City Paper*, September 25–October 2, 1997.

43. Allen Ginsberg, "Howl," in *Howl and Other Poems* (San Francisco: City Lights Books, 1957).

44. Nelson, "Punk Poet Speaks."

45. DeLano, "Torch Singer."

46. The socks are not inexpensive.

47. Patti Smith, "The Girl of Flanders," introduction to *Ann Demeulemeester*, by Ann Demeulemeester (New York: Rizzoli, 2014), 5.

48. Ann Demeulemeester as told to Laird Borrelli-Persson, " 'Our Body Is the Most Sophisticated Machine': Ann Demeulemeester on the Resonance of Her 'Corps Humain' Collection in the Age of COVID," *Vogue*, December 26, 2020.

49. Wanda M. Corn, *Georgia O'Keeffe: Living Modern* (New York: DelMonico Books / Prestel, 2017), 141.

50. Tessa Stuart, "Elizabeth Warren: The *Rolling Stone* Interview," *Rolling Stone*, December 19, 2019.

51. Jody Denberg, "*Gung Ho*: Patti Smith," *Austin Chronicle*, March 31, 2000.

52. Ibid.

53. Check them out on YouTube; they are incredibly heartwarming.

54. "I Am Lilith, Hear Me Roar . . . ," *Los Angeles Times*, April 13, 1998.

55. Smith, *Just Kids*, 244.

5. Blue Star

1. Vanessa Grigoriadis, "Remembrances of the Punk Prose Poetess," *New York*, January 7, 2010.

2. Brian McCollum, "Patti Smith's Valentine: A Night of Music, Reading and Family at the DIA," *Detroit Free Press*, February 14, 2018.

3. Alice O'Keeffe, "*M Train* by Patti Smith Review: Into the Mind of an Artist," *Guardian*, November 19, 2015.

4. Michiko Kakutani, "Review: 'M Train,' Patti Smith on All the Roads She Has Taken," *New York Times*, October 1, 2015.

5. "The Best Music Books of 2019," *Pitchfork*, December 19, 2019, https://pitchfork.com/features/lists-and-guides/best-music-books-2019/.

6. Robert Christgau, "Patti Smith: Save This Rock and Roll Hero," *Village Voice*, January 17, 1977.

7. Patti Smith, "Twin Death," in *9.11 Babelogue* (New York: Bertha and Karl Leubsdorf Art Gallery at Hunter College, 2011), 9.

8. Ed Vulliamy, " 'Some give a song. Some give a life . . . ,' " *Guardian*, June 3, 2005.

9. Caroline Sullivan, "Songs of Experience," *Guardian*, June 28, 2005.

10. It was recorded and released as the second disc in a Sony Legacy edition of the record released later that year.

11. There is some weird math involved in this calculation. I took this from the Hall of Fame website, www.rockhall.com/.

12. Lenny Kaye has been a member of the nominating committee since 1987.

13. Patti Smith, "Ain't It Strange?," *New York Times*, March 12, 2007.

14. Ibid.

15. Video of de la Rocha's induction speech and Patti Smith's acceptance speech is available on the page dedicated to her on the Rock & Roll Hall of Fame website, http://rockhall.com/inductees/patti-smith.

16. Ibid.

17. Ibid.

18. Keith Richards was in the house to induct the Ronettes.

19. Bob Lefsetz, "Patti Smith," *Lefsetz Letter*, January 13, 2007, https://lefsetz.com/wordpress/2007/01/13/patti-smith/.

20. Bob Lefsetz, "Bad Company at the L.A. County Fair," *Lefsetz Letter*, September 5, 2016, https://lefsetz.com/wordpress/2016/09/05/bad-company-l-county-fair/.

21. Bob Lefsetz, "Patti Smith in the *New York Times*," *Lefsetz Letter*, March 12, 2007, https://lefsetz.com/wordpress/2007/03/12/patti-smith-in-the-new-york-times/.

22. Mary Beard, *Women and Power: A Manifesto* (New York: Liveright, 2017), 4, 8, Kindle edition.

23. Ibid., 5.

24. Interview with the author, January 2021.

25. Alice Vincent, "Patti Smith at Glastonbury 2015 Review," *Telegraph*, June 28, 2015.

26. Now the Museum of Pop Culture.

27. In 2007, of course, she covered "Smells Like Teen Spirit" for *Twelve*; I still prefer her rendition of "Heart-Shaped Box."

28. Patti Smith, "How Does It Feel," *New Yorker*, December 14, 2016.

29. Ibid.

30. Ibid.

31. Jerry Portwood, "The Last Word: Patti Smith on Performing with Her Kids and What William Burroughs Taught Her," *Rolling Stone*, December 7, 2018.